EASY PIANO
Choice JAZZ Standards

ISBN 0-7935-8331-4

HAL•LEONARD®
CORPORATION

7777 W. BLUEMOUND RD. P.O. BOX 13819 MILWAUKEE, WI 53213

Visit Hal Leonard Online at
www.halleonard.com

EASY PIANO
Choice JAZZ Standards

ANGEL EYES

Words by EARL BRENT
Music by MATT DENNIS

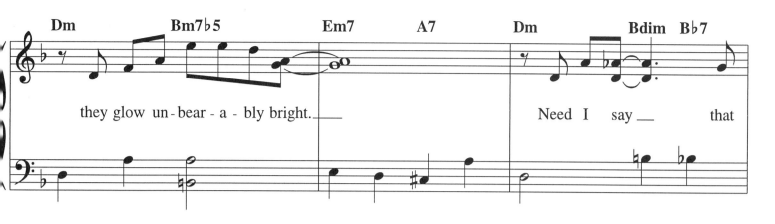
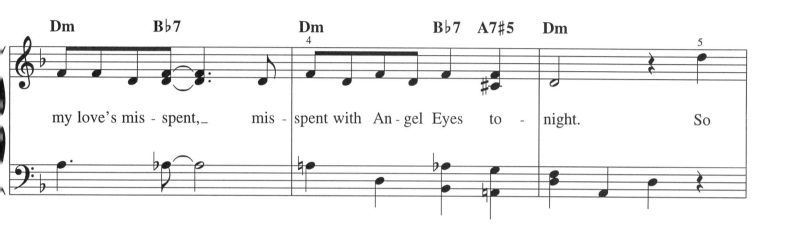
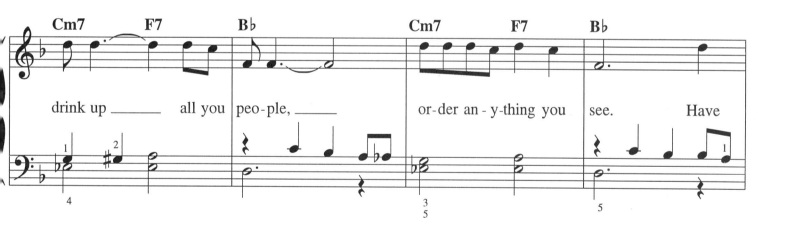
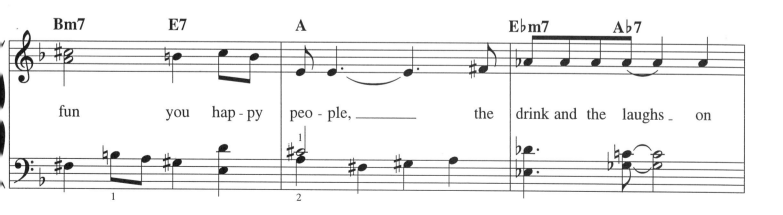

me.   Par - don   me, ___   but   I   got - ta   run,

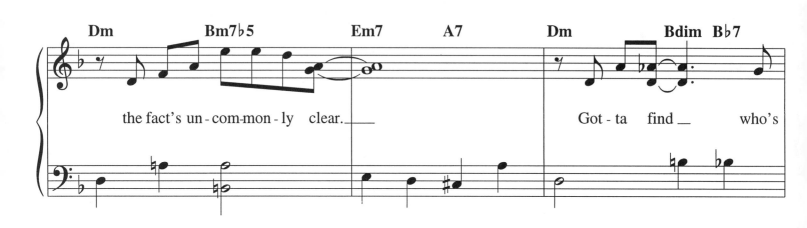

the fact's un - com - mon - ly   clear. ___   Got - ta   find ___   who's

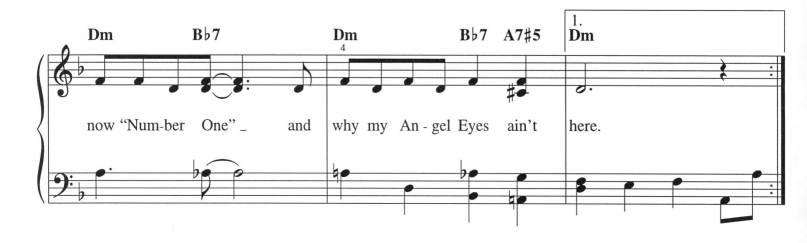

now "Num - ber   One" _   and   why my An - gel Eyes   ain't   here.

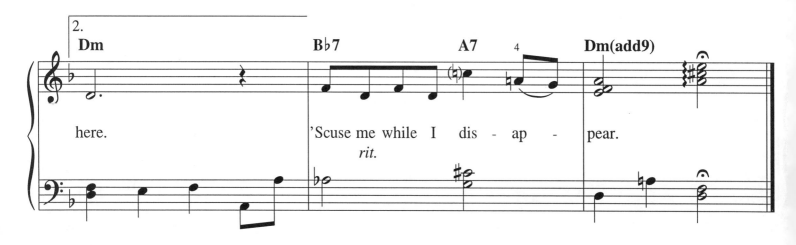

here.   'Scuse me while I   dis - ap - pear.
rit.

AUTUMN IN NEW YORK

Words and Music by
VERNON DUKE

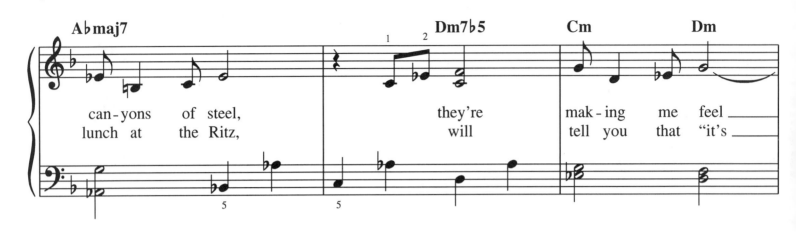

can-yons   of steel,   they're   mak-ing   me   feel
lunch at   the Ritz,   will   tell you   that "it's

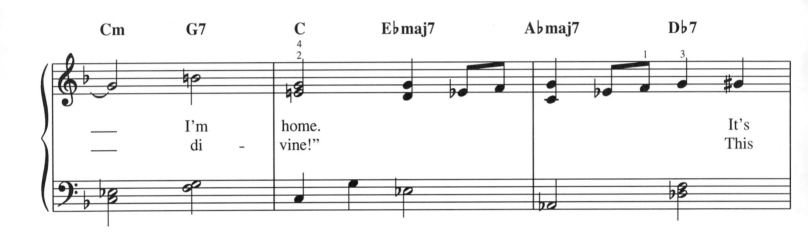

___   I'm   home.   It's
___   di -   vine!"   This

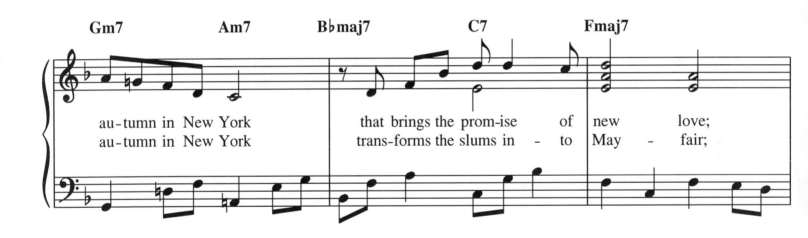

au-tumn in New York   that brings the prom-ise   of   new   love;
au-tumn in New York   trans-forms the slums in - to   May -   fair;

Au-tumn in New York   is   of-ten min-gled with
Au-tumn in New York   you'll need no cas-tles   in

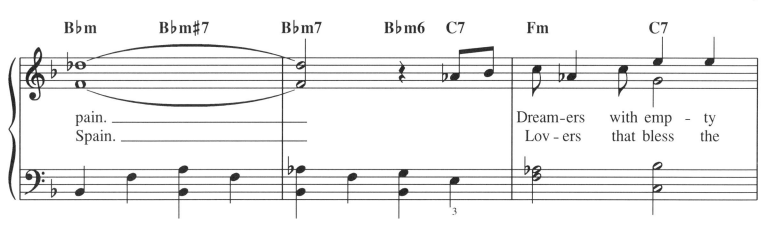

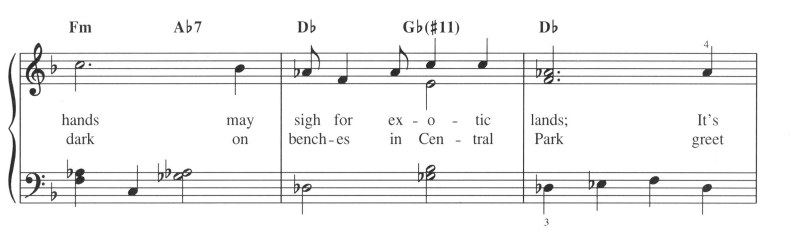

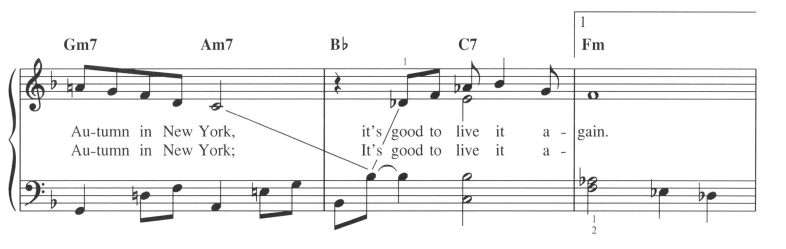

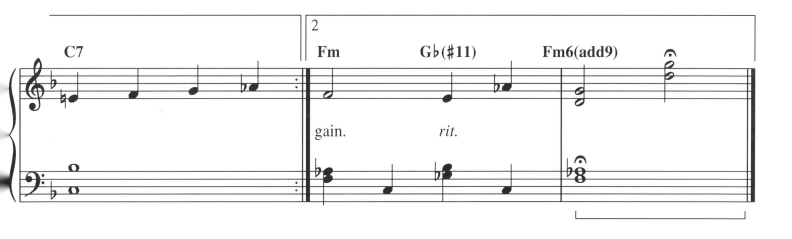

THE BLUE ROOM
from THE GIRL FRIEND

Words by LORENZ HART
Music by RICHARD RODGERS

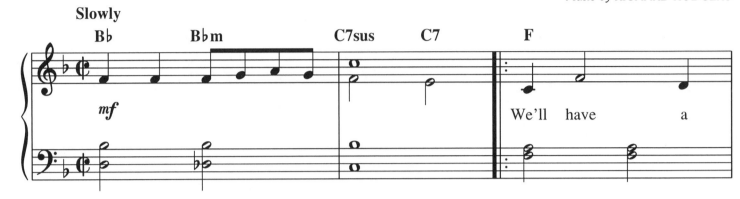

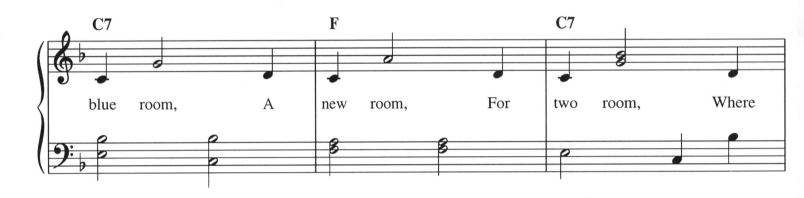

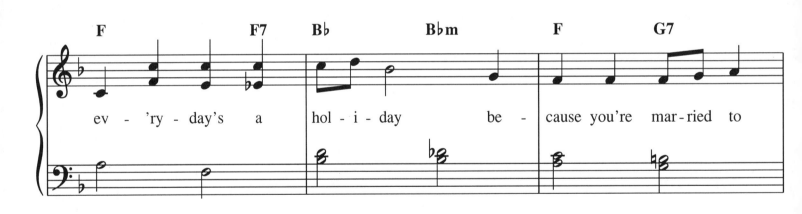

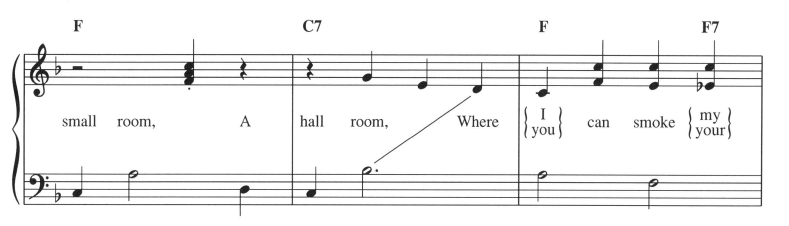

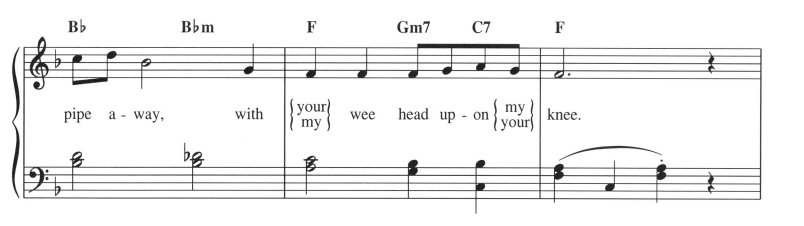

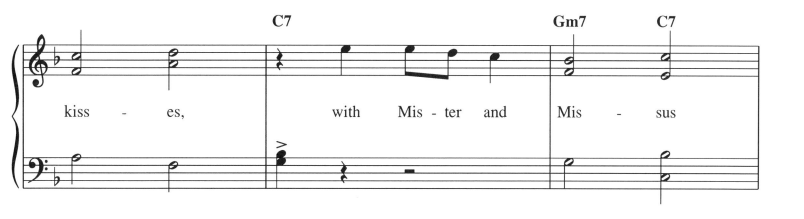

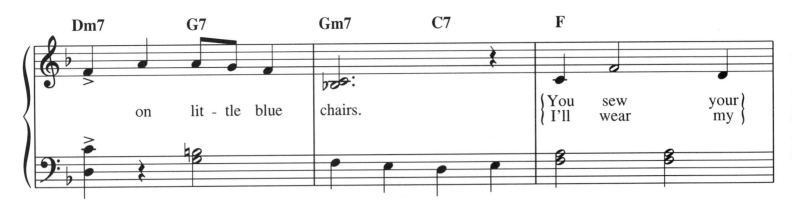

on lit - tle blue chairs.

{You sew your}
{I'll wear my}

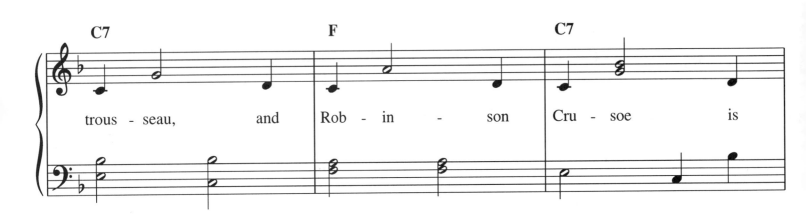

trous - seau, and Rob - in - son Cru - soe is

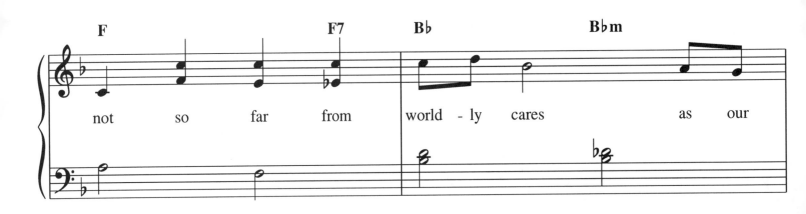

not so far from world - ly cares as our

blue room far a - way up - stairs!

1.
stairs!

2.
stairs!

CHEEK TO CHEEK

from the RKO Radio Motion Picture TOP HAT

Words and Music by
IRVING BERLIN

Heav - en, _____ I'm in Heav - en, _____
Heav - en, _____ I'm in Heav - en, _____

_____ And my heart beats so that I can hard - ly
_____ And the cares that hung a - round me thru the

speak; _____ And I seem to find the
week _____ Seem to van - ish like a

© Copyright 1935 by Irving Berlin
Copyright Renewed
International Copyright Secured   All Rights Reserved

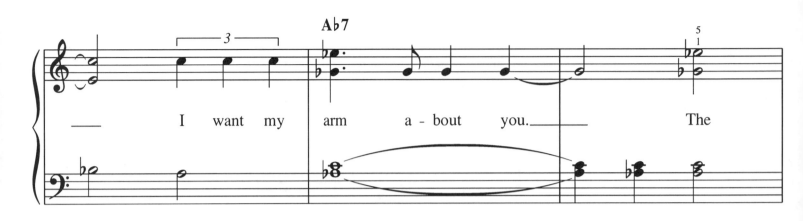

I want my arm a-bout you. The

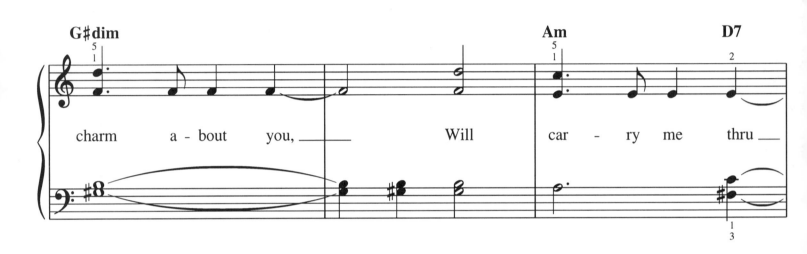

charm a-bout you, Will car - ry me thru

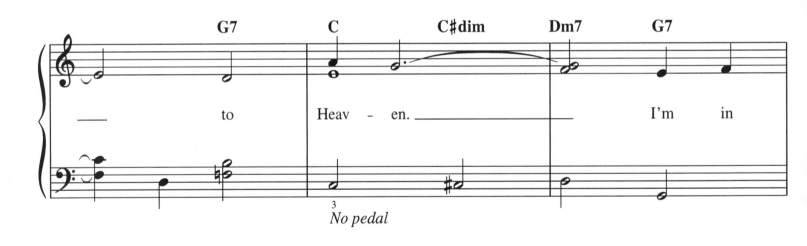

to Heav - en. I'm in

No pedal

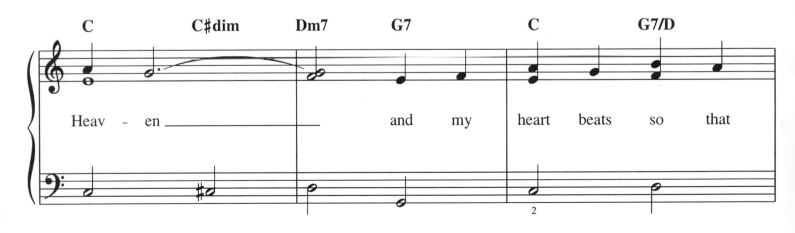

Heav - en and my heart beats so that

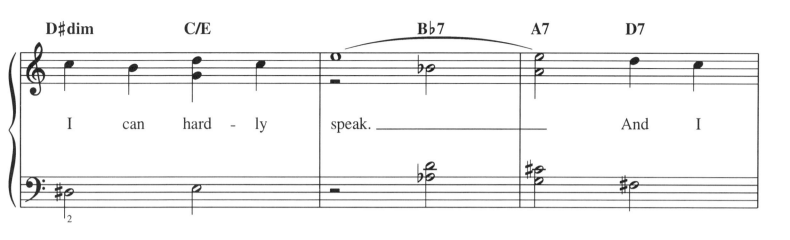

I can hard - ly speak. _____ And I

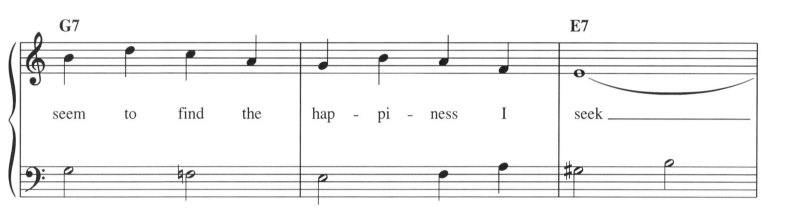

seem to find the hap - pi - ness I seek _____

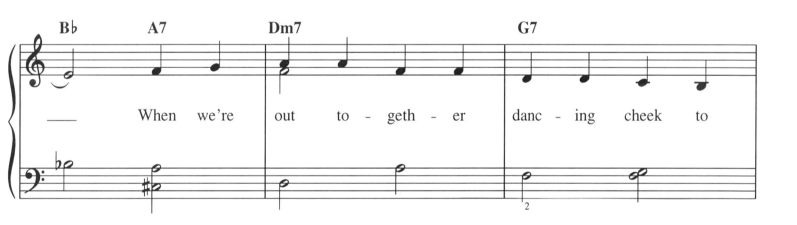

___ When we're out to - geth - er danc - ing cheek to

cheek. _____

CARAVAN
from SOPHISTICATED LADIES

Words and Music by DUKE ELLINGTON,
IRVING MILLS and JUAN TIZOL

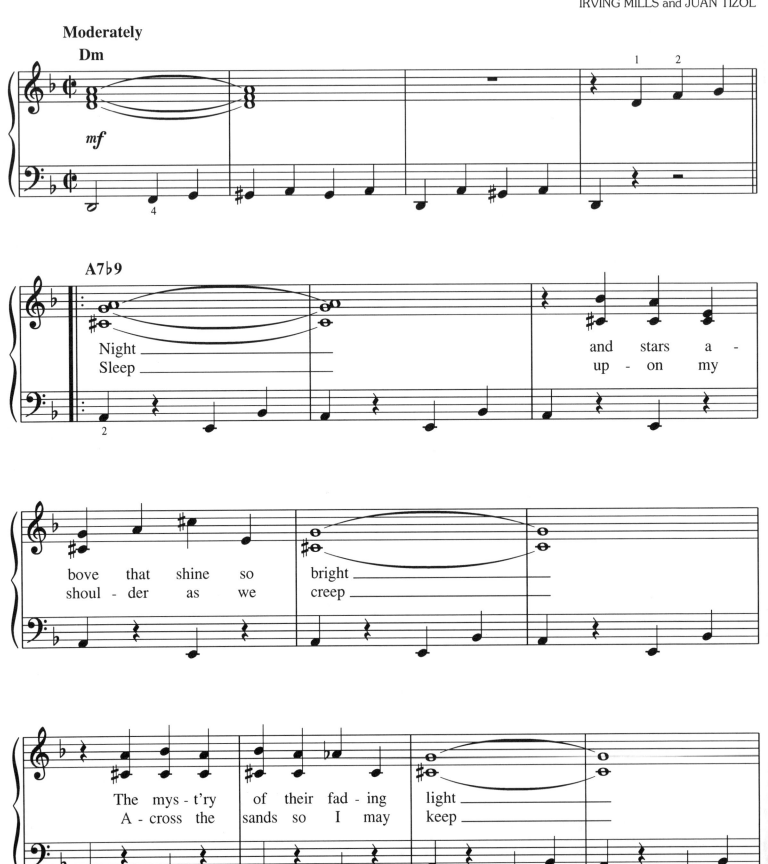

that shines up - on our car - a - van; ____
This mem - 'ry of our car - a - van. ____

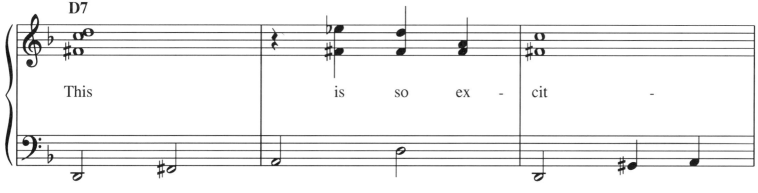

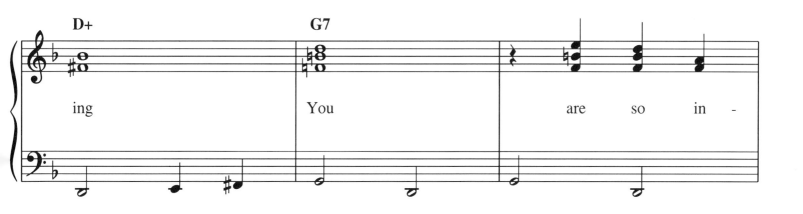

This is so ex - cit - ing You are so in -

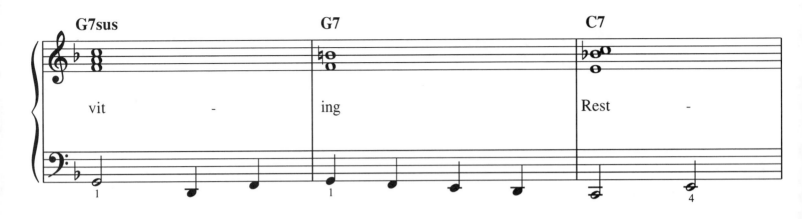

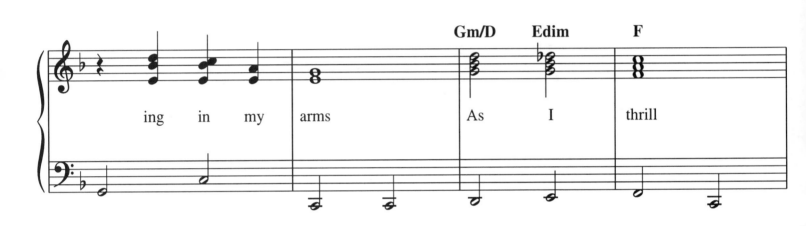

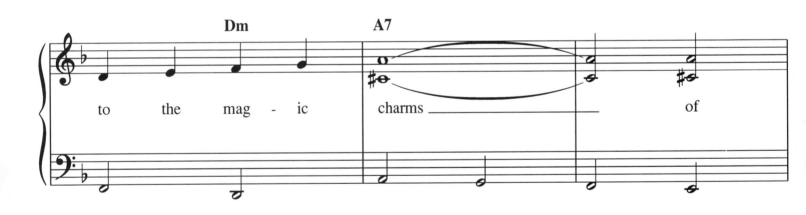

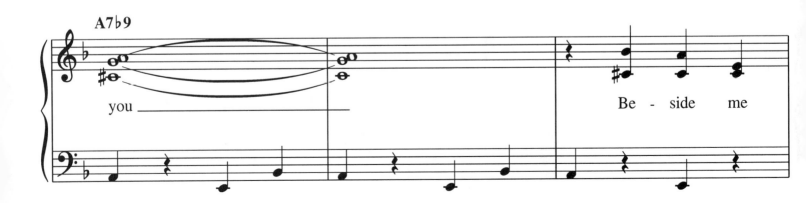

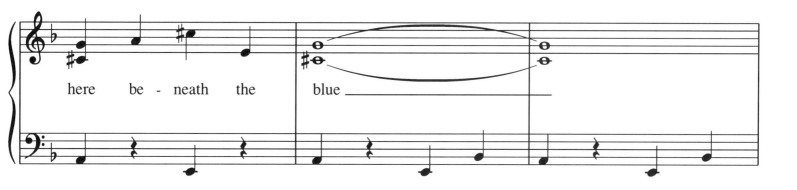

here be - neath the blue _____

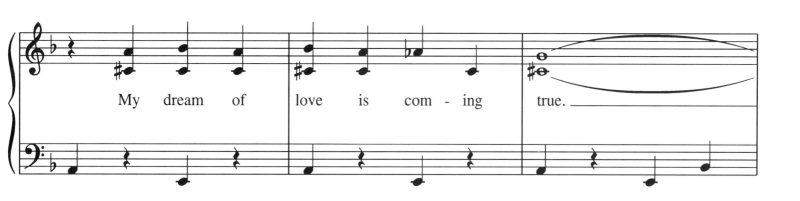

My dream of love is com - ing true. _____

_____ With - in our des - ert car - a -

Dm6

van. _____

CHEROKEE
(Indian Love Song)

Words and Music by
RAY NOBLE

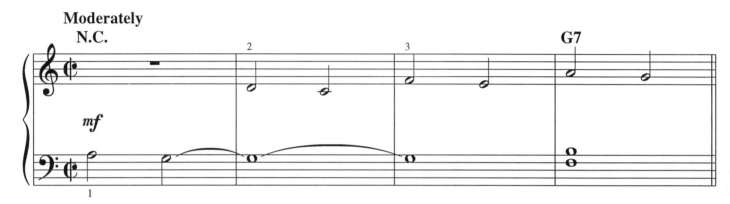

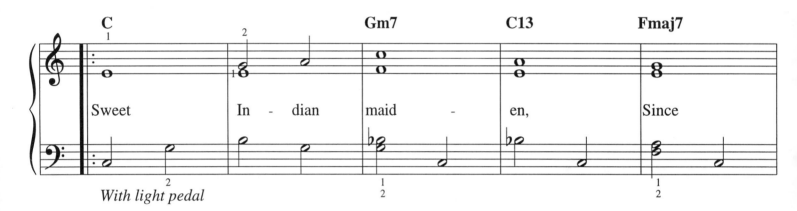

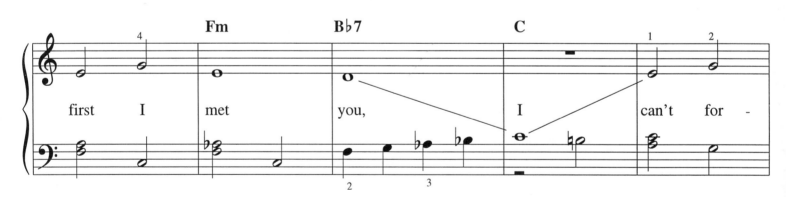

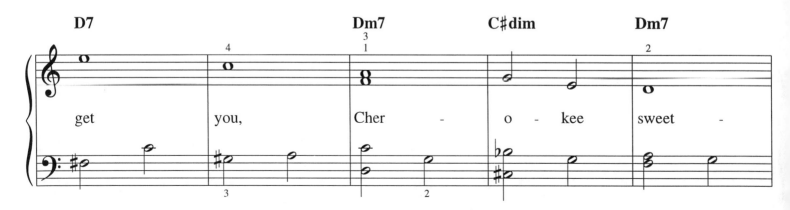

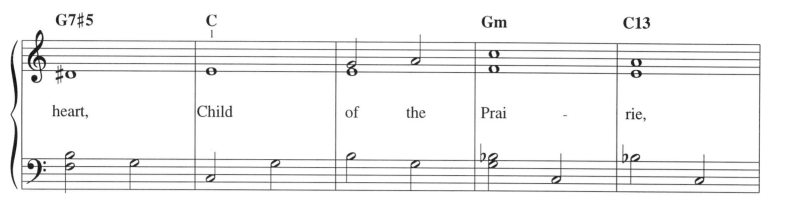

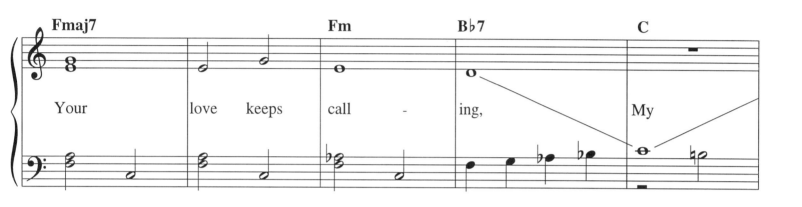

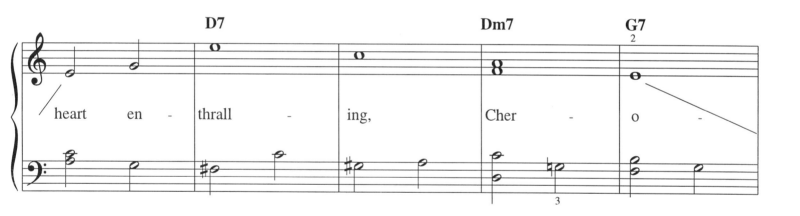

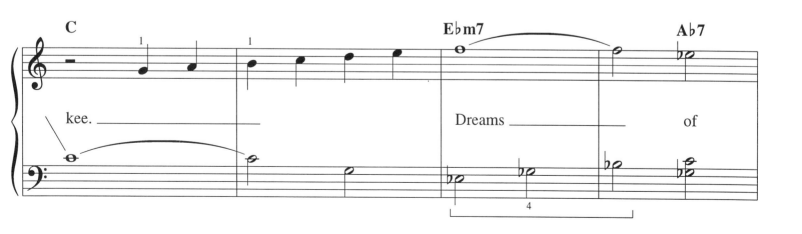

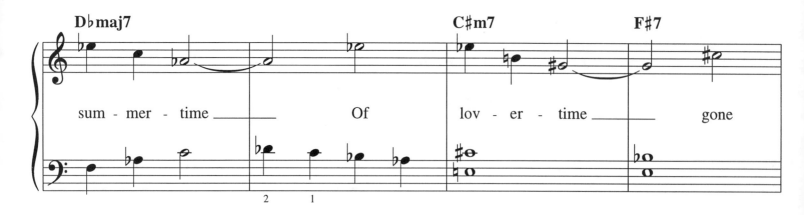

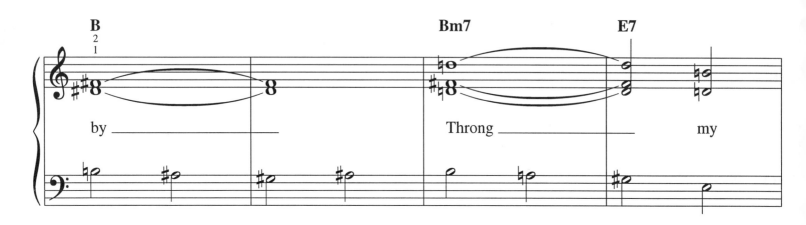

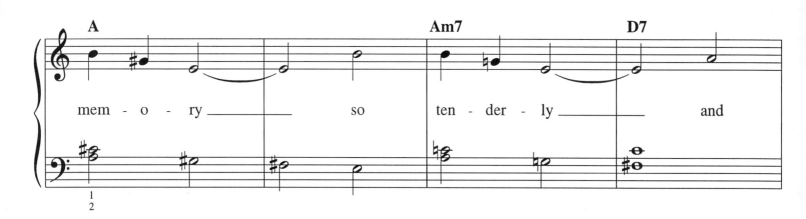

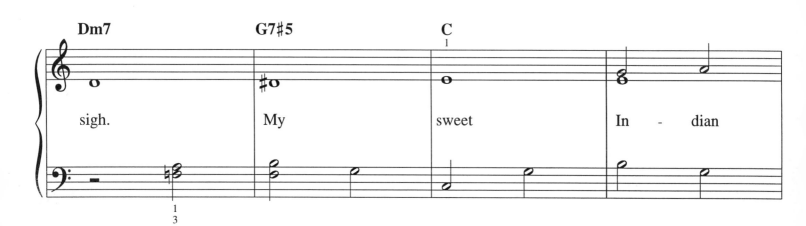

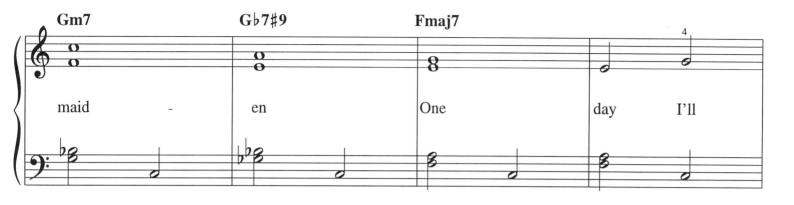

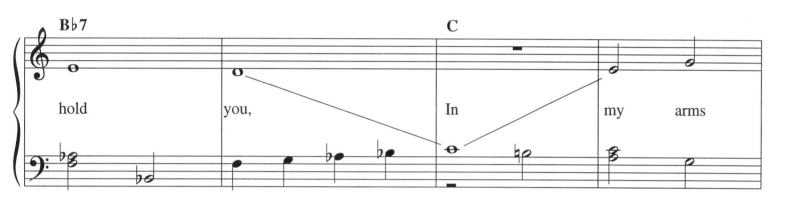

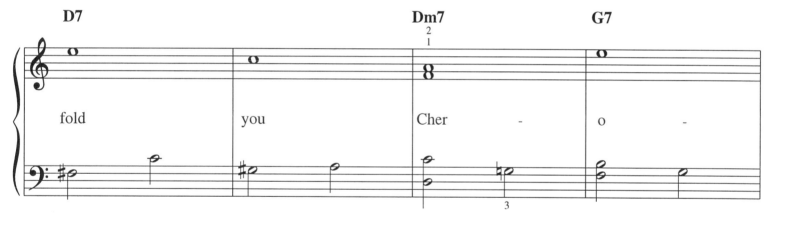

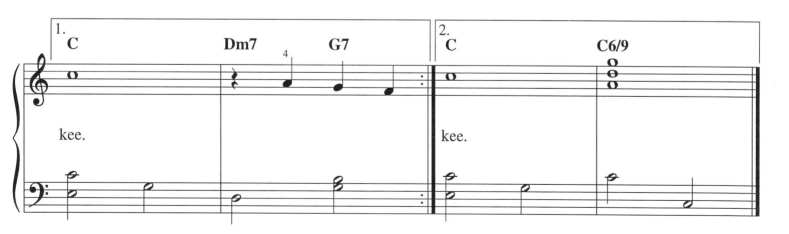

A FINE ROMANCE
from SWING TIME

Words by DOROTHY FIELDS
Music by JEROME KERN

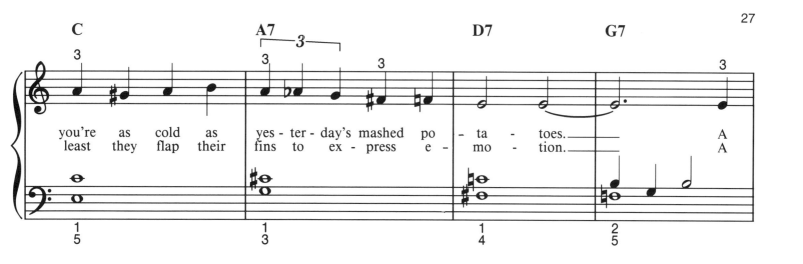

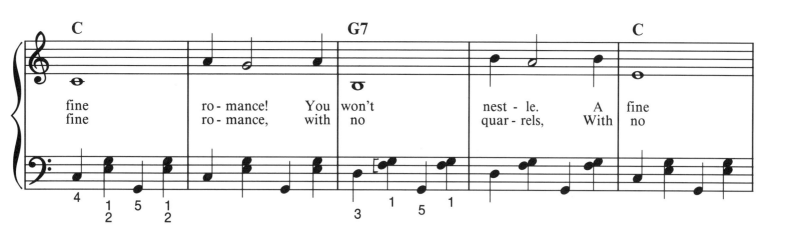

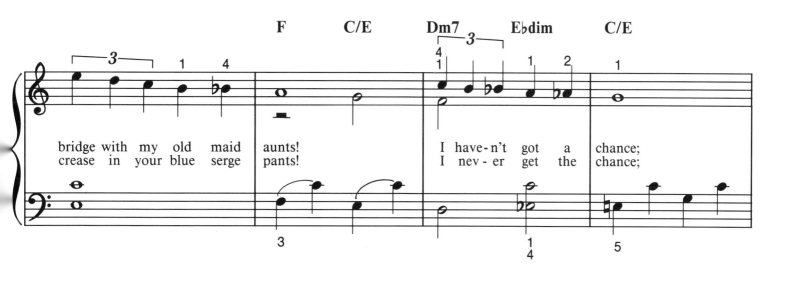

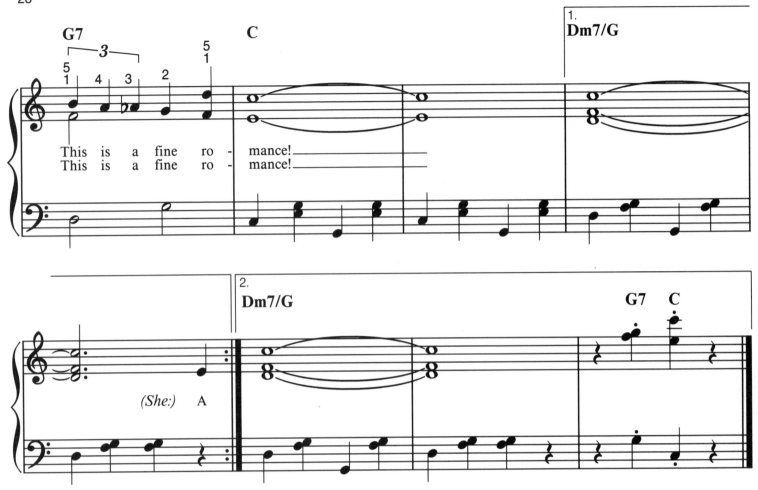

This is a fine ro - mance!_____
This is a fine ro - mance!_____

(She:) A

Additional Words

She:
A fine romance,
With no kisses!
A fine romance,
My friend, this is!
We two should be like clams in a dish of chowder;
But we just fizz like parts of a Seidlitz Powder.
A fine romance
With no clinches,
A fine romance
With no pinches.
You're just as hard to land as the "Ile de France!"
I haven't got a chance.
This is a fine romance!

He:
A fine romance
My dear duchess,
Two old fogies
Who need crutches!
True love should have the thrills that a healthy crime has!
We don't have half the thrills that the "March of Time" has!
A fine romance,
My good woman,
My strong "aged in the wood" woman!
You never give the orchids I sent a glance!
No! You like cactus plants,
This is a fine romance.

THE GLORY OF LOVE

Words and Music by
BILLY HILL

Be - fore the clouds roll by a lit - tle That's the sto - ry of,

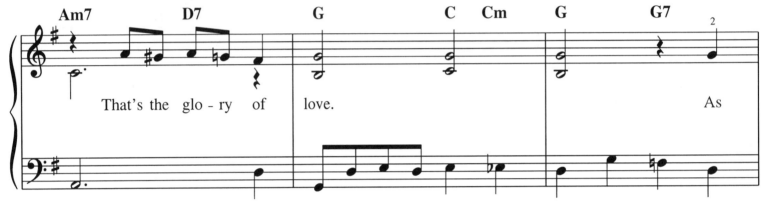

That's the glo - ry of love. As

long as there's the two of us we've got the world and all its

No pedal

charms And when the world is through with us

GOOD MORNING HEARTACHE

Words and Music by DAN FISHER,
IRENE HIGGINBOTHAM and ERVIN DRAKE

Slowly

With pedal

Good morn-ing heart-ache, you old gloom-y sight, Good morn-ing heart-ache, tho't we

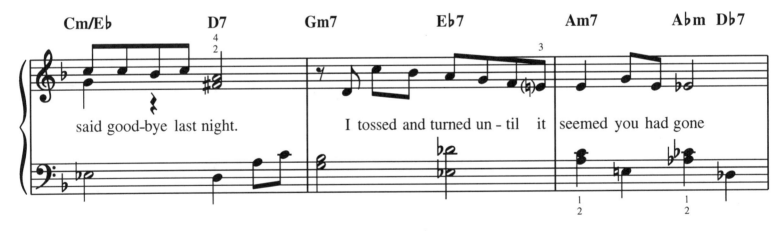

said good-bye last night. I tossed and turned un-til it seemed you had gone

But here you are with the dawn, Wish I'd for-get you

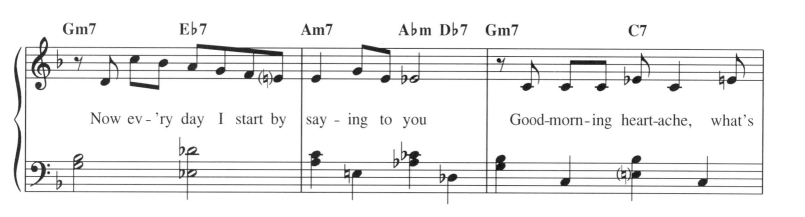

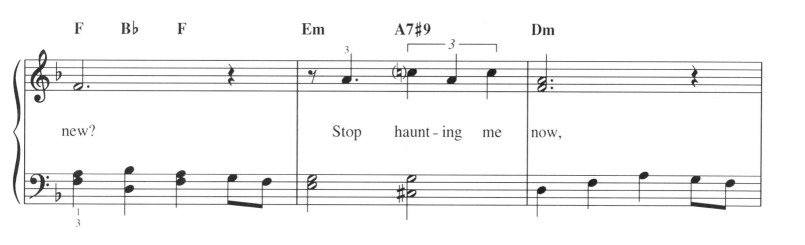

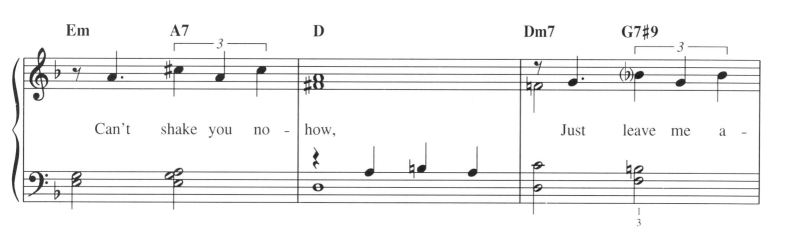

lone　　　　　　　　I've got those Mon-day blues straight thru Sun-day blues.

Good morn-ing heart-ache　　here we go a-gain,　　Good morn-ing heart-ache you're the

one who knew me when,　　Might as well get used to you　hang-in' a-round,

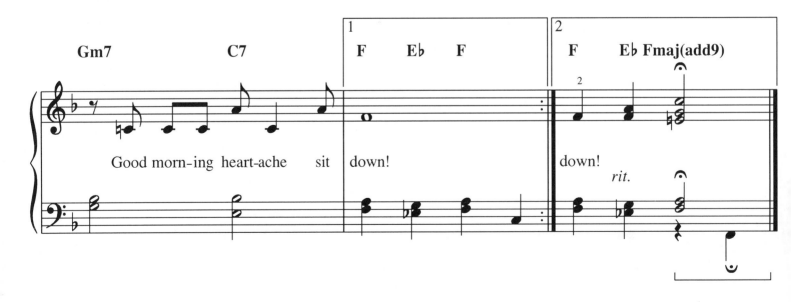

Good morn-ing heart-ache　sit down!　　　down!

HOW DEEP IS THE OCEAN
(How High Is the Sky)

Words and Music by
IRVING BERLIN

Moderately

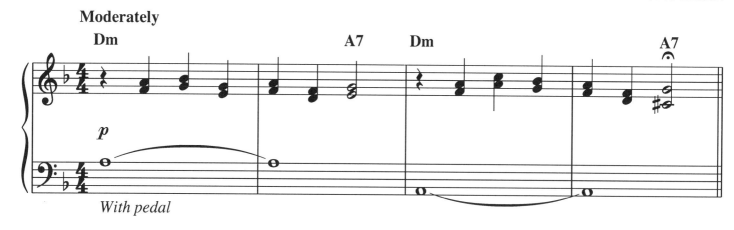

With pedal

How much do I love you? I'll tell you no

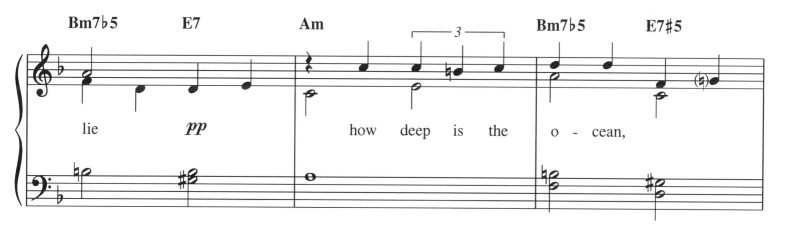

lie *pp* how deep is the o - cean,

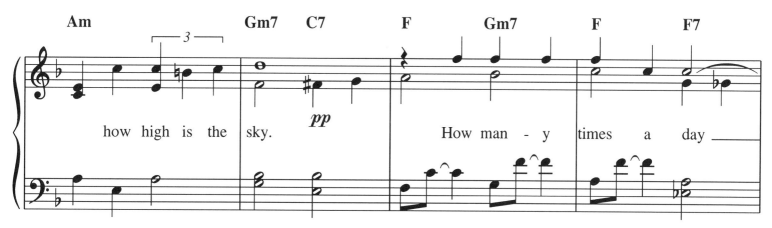

how high is the sky. *pp* How man - y times a day ___

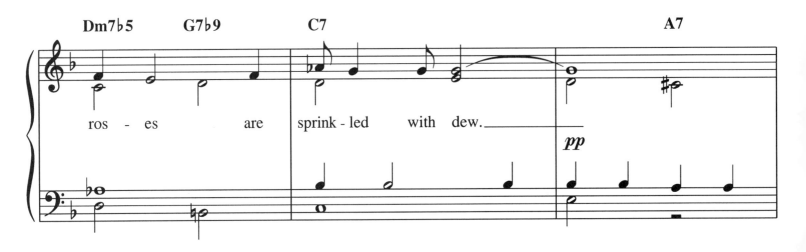

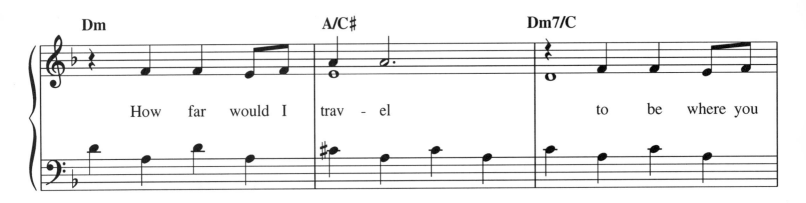

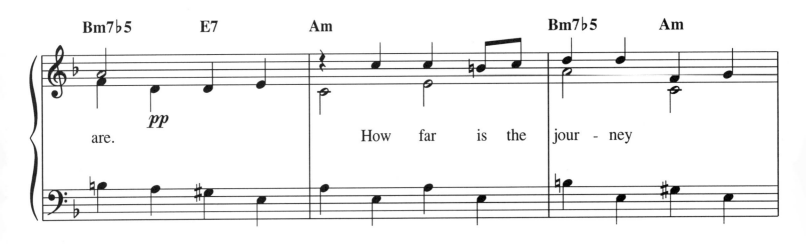

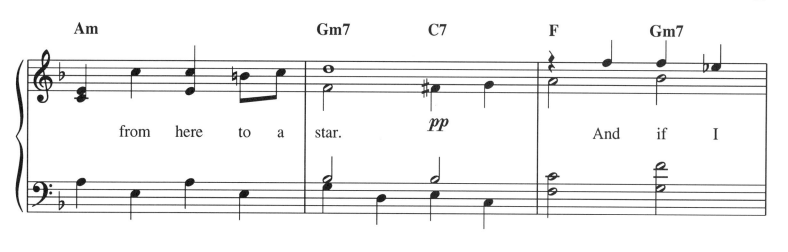

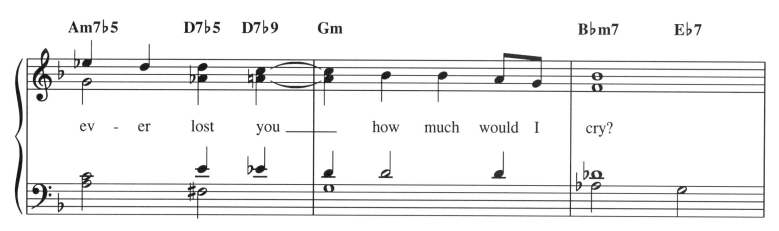

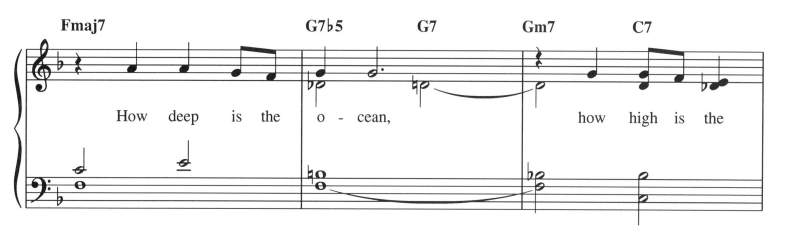

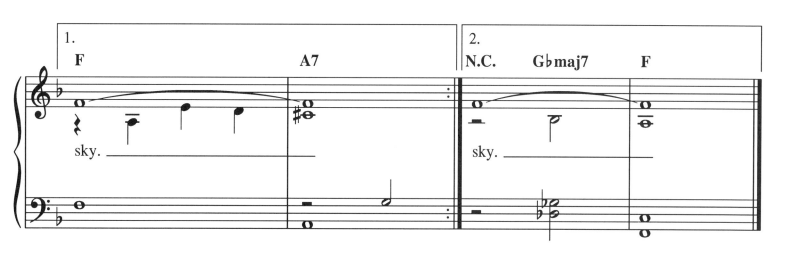

I COULD WRITE A BOOK

from PAL JOEY

Words by LORENZ HART
Music by RICHARD RODGERS

If they asked me I could write a book, _____

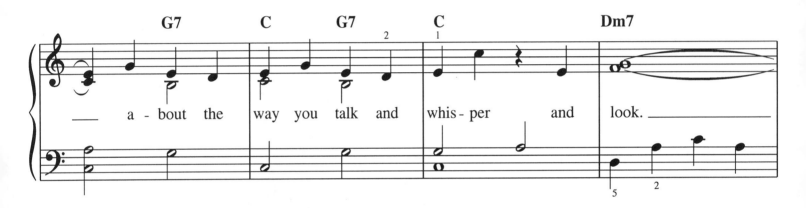

_____ a - bout the way you talk and whis - per and look. _____

_____ I could write a pre - face on how we

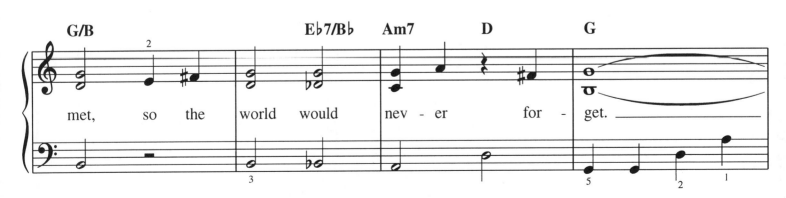

met, so the world would nev - er for - get. _____

39

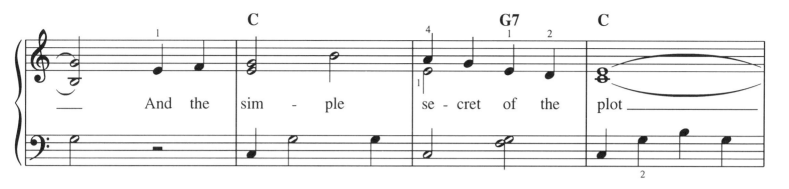

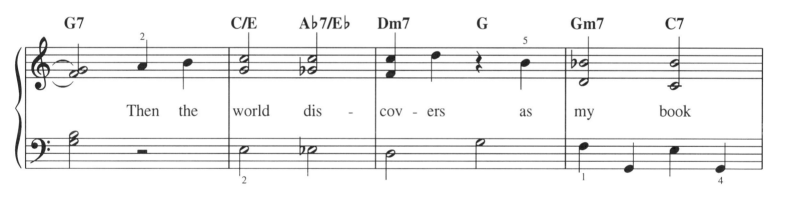

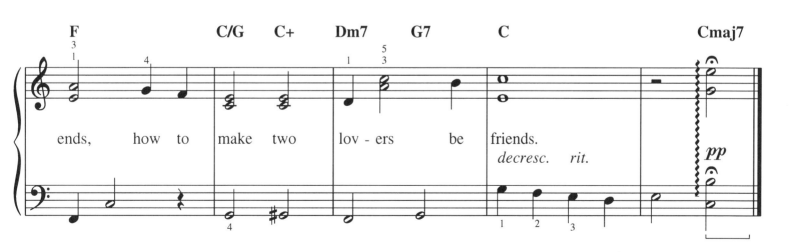

I WON'T DANCE

from ROBERTA

Lyrics by OSCAR HAMMERSTEIN II and OTTO HARBACH
Screen Version by DOROTHY FIELDS and JIMMY McHUGH
Music by JEROME KERN

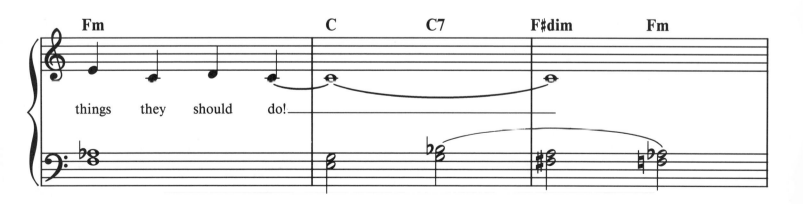

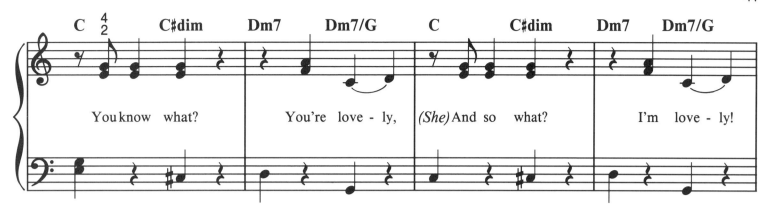

You know what? You're love - ly, *(She)* And so what? I'm love - ly!

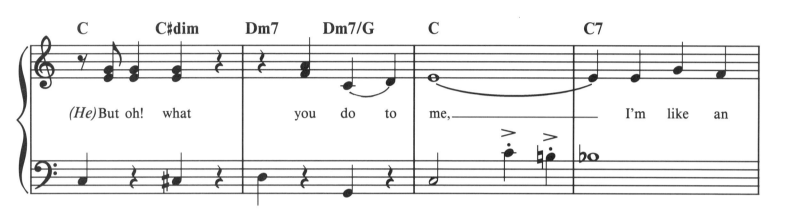

(He) But oh! what you do to me, I'm like an

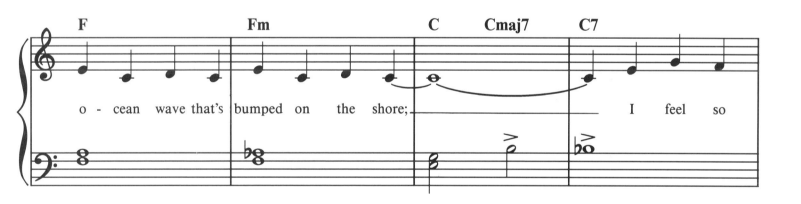

o - cean wave that's bumped on the shore; I feel so

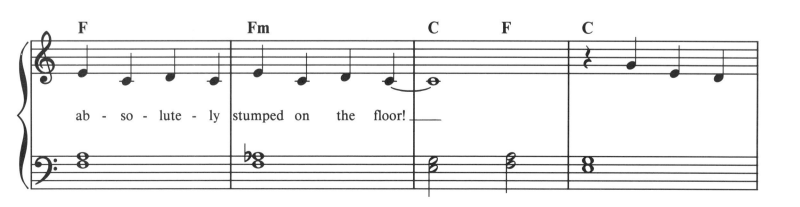

ab - so - lute - ly stumped on the floor!

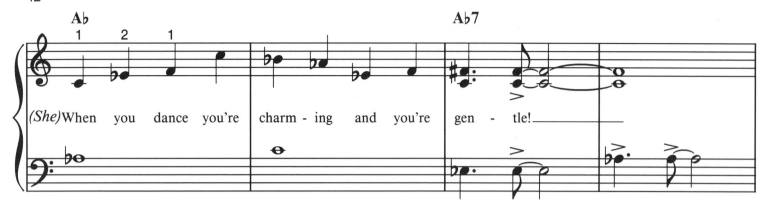

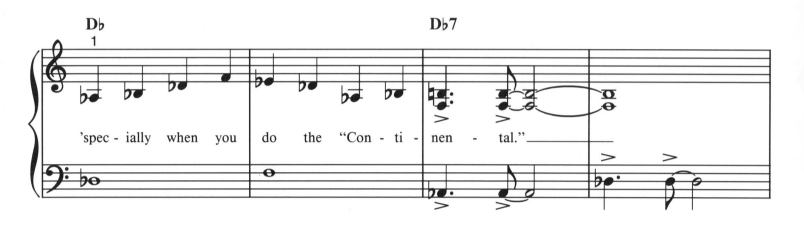

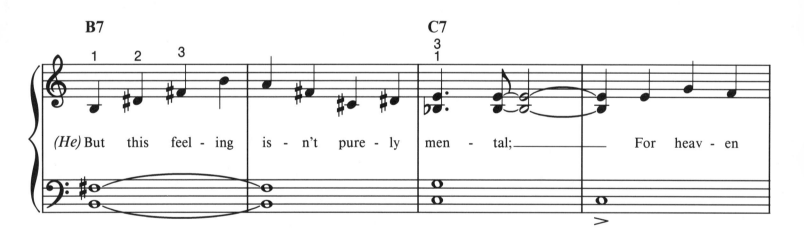

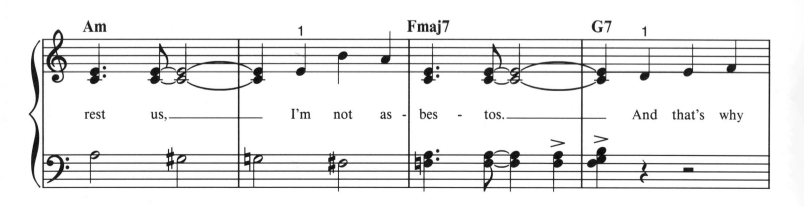

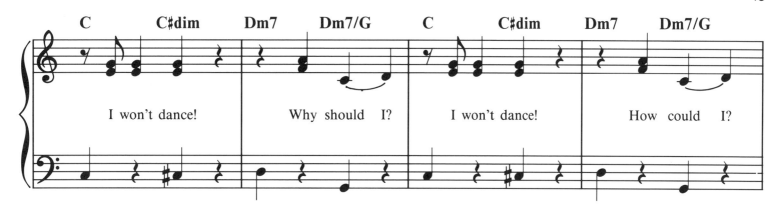

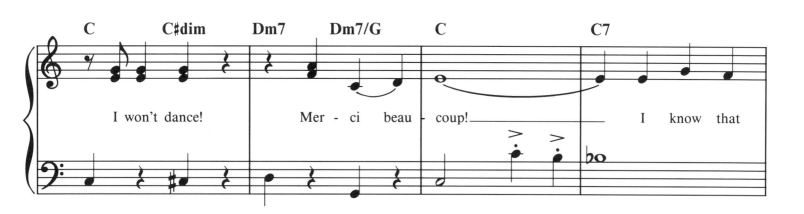

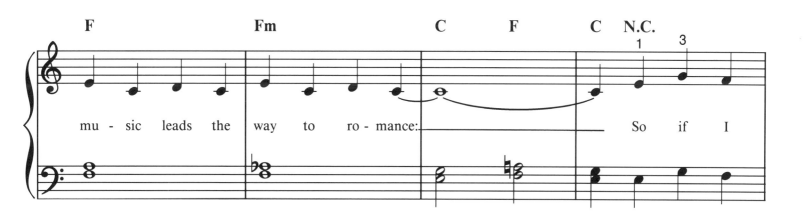

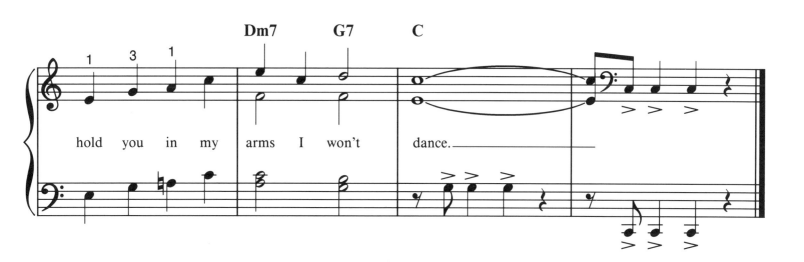

IF I WERE A BELL

from GUYS AND DOLLS

By FRANK LOESSER

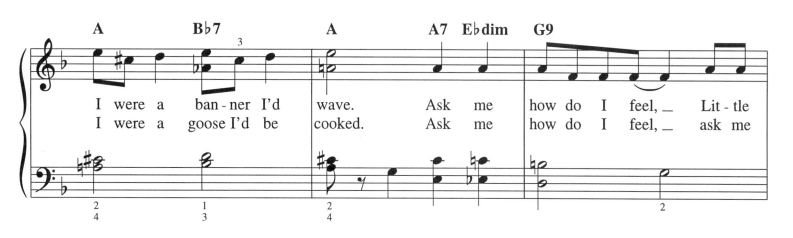

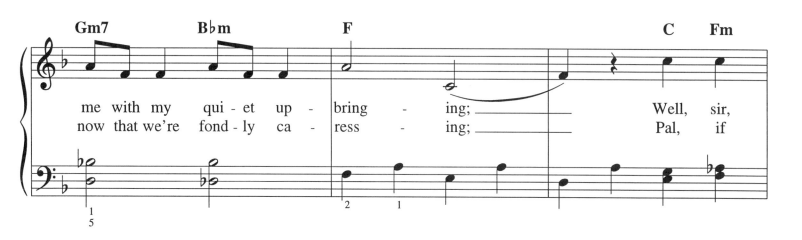

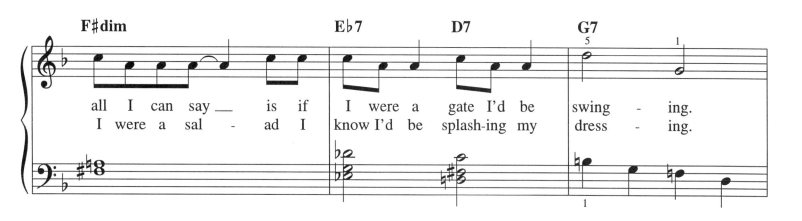

46

IT MIGHT AS WELL BE SPRING

from STATE FAIR

Lyrics by OSCAR HAMMERSTEIN II
Music by RICHARD RODGERS

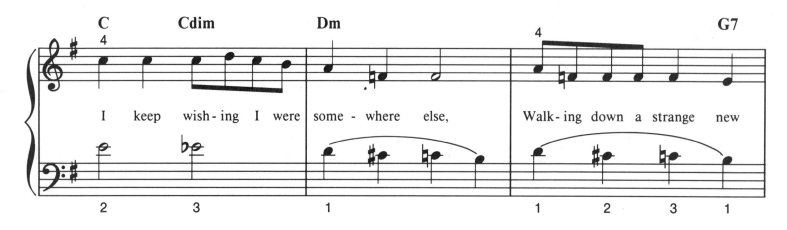

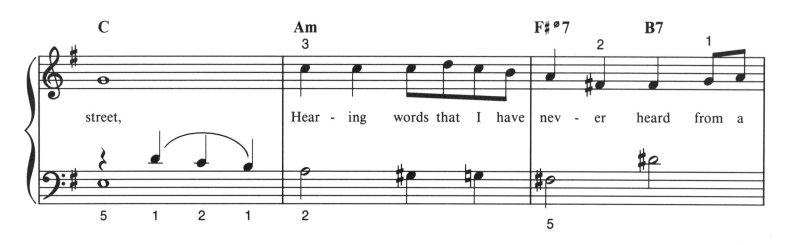

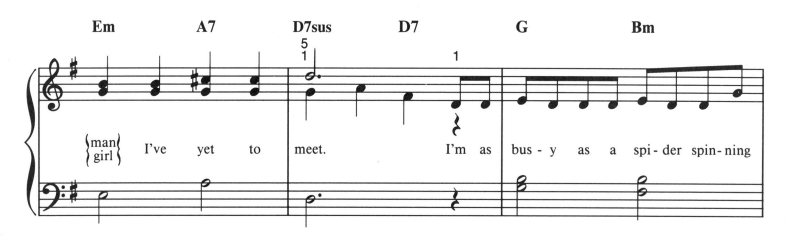

49

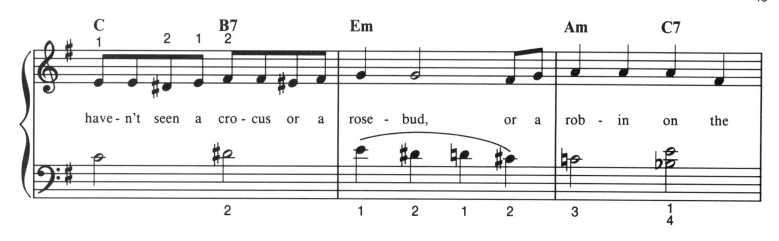

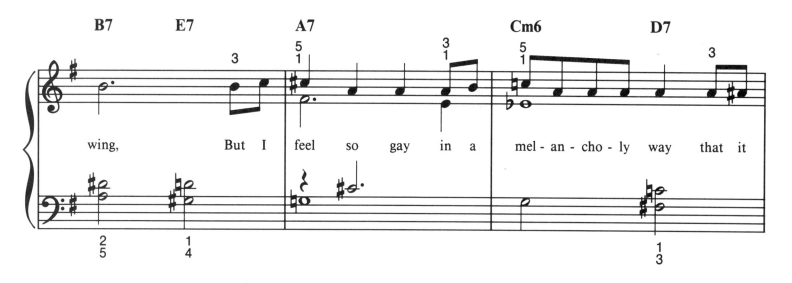

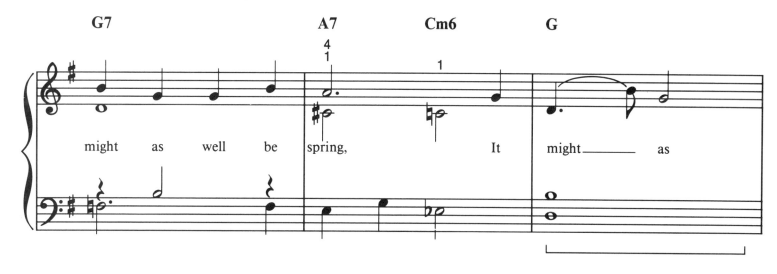

IN THE WEE SMALL
HOURS OF THE MORNING

Words by BOB HILLIARD
Music by DAVID MANN

JUNE IN JANUARY
from the Paramount Picture HERE IS MY HEART

Words and Music by LEO ROBIN
and RALPH RAINGER

Moderately slow

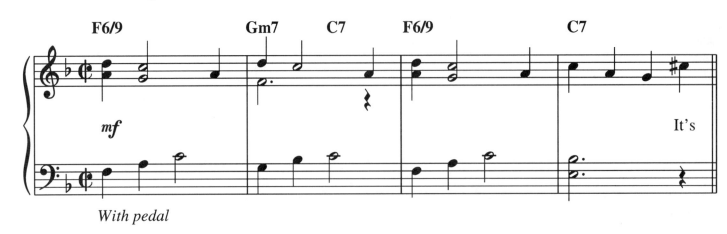

mf

With pedal

It's

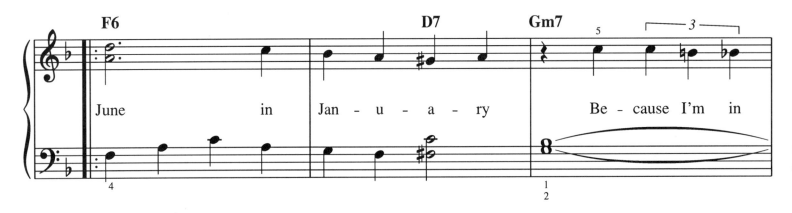

June   in   Jan - u - a - ry   Be - cause I'm in

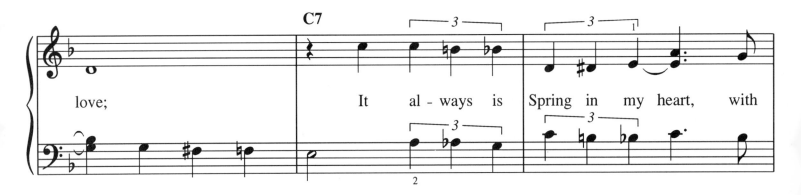

love;   It al - ways is Spring in my heart,   with

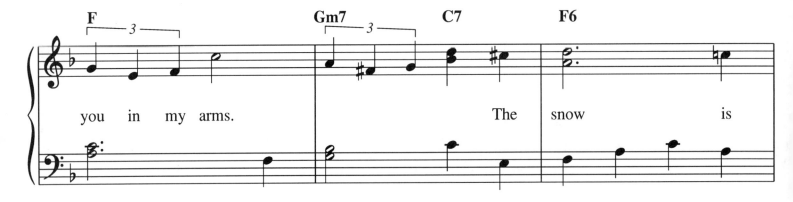

you in my arms.   The   snow   is

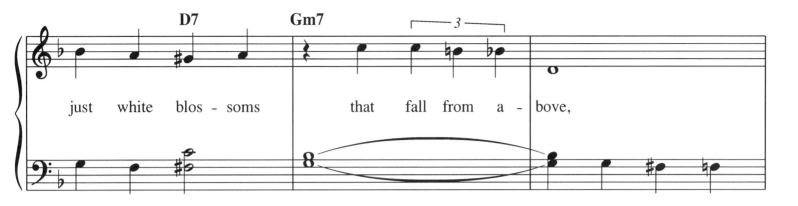

just white blos - soms   that fall from a - bove,

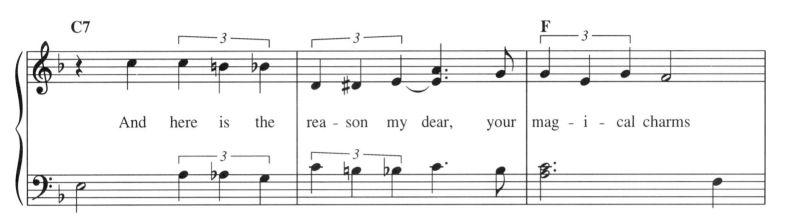

And here is the rea - son my dear, your mag - i - cal charms

The night is cold

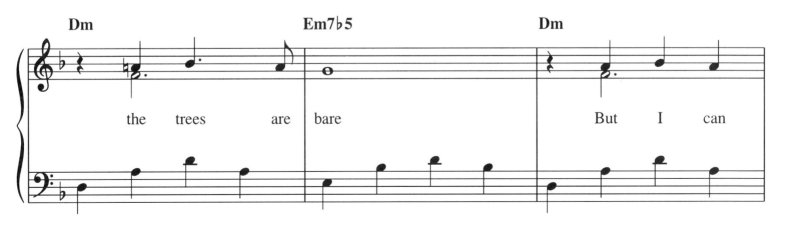

the trees are bare   But I can

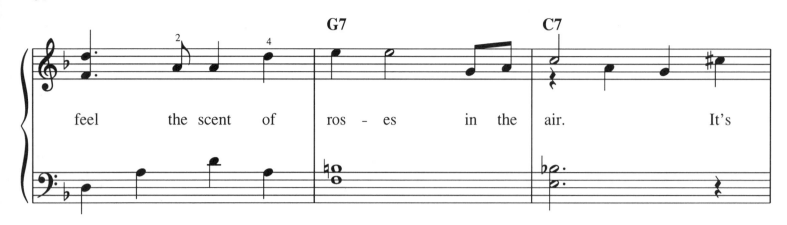

feel   the scent   of   ros – es   in   the   air.   It's

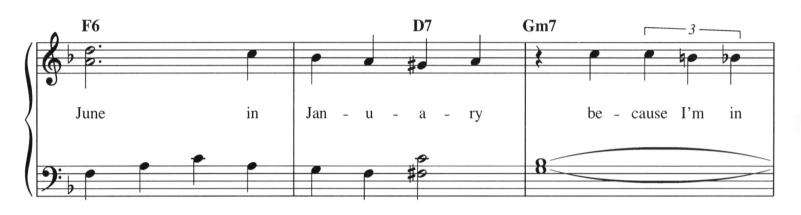

June   in   Jan – u – a – ry   be – cause I'm   in

love,   But   on – ly   be – cause I'm   in   love   with

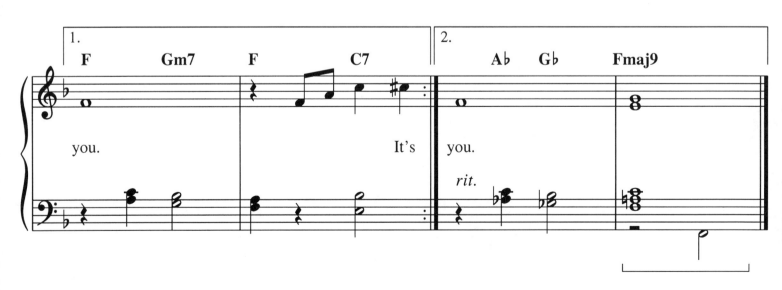

you.   It's   you.

MAKIN' WHOOPEE!
from WHOOPEE!

Lyrics by GUS KAHN
Music by WALTER DONALDSON

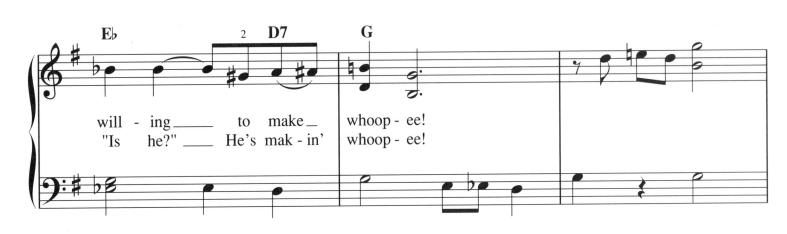

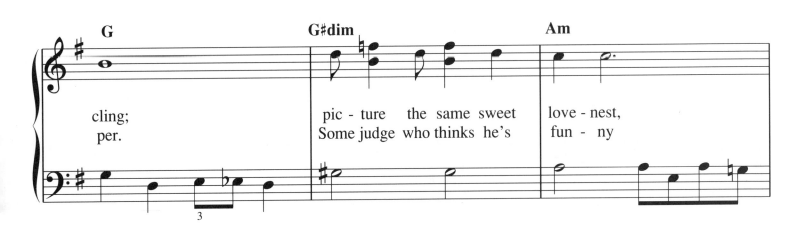

think what a year can bring. _____ He's wash-ing dish-es _____ and ba-by
says, "You'll pay six to her. _____ He says,"Now judge, _____ sup-pose I

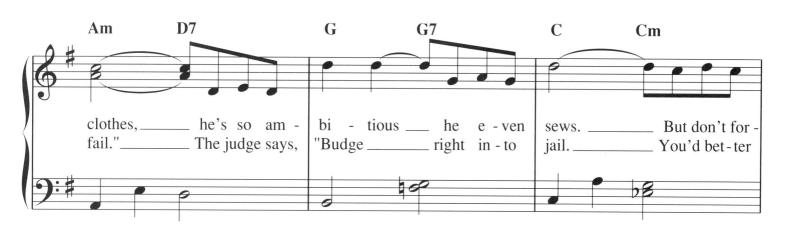

clothes, _____ he's so am - bi - tious _____ he e-ven sews. _____ But don't for -
fail." _____ The judge says, "Budge _____ right in-to jail. _____ You'd bet-ter

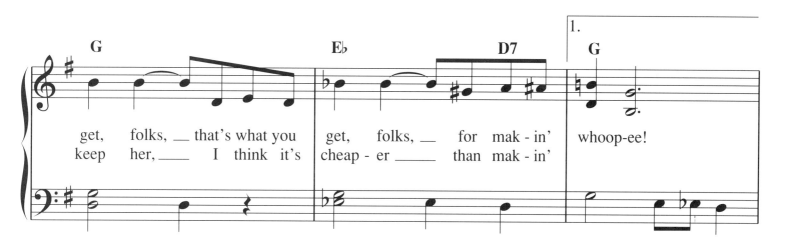

get, folks, __ that's what you get, folks, __ for mak-in' whoop-ee!
keep her, __ I think it's cheap-er _____ than mak-in'

An - oth - er whoop-ee!"

LOLLIPOPS AND ROSES

Words and Music by
TONY VELONA

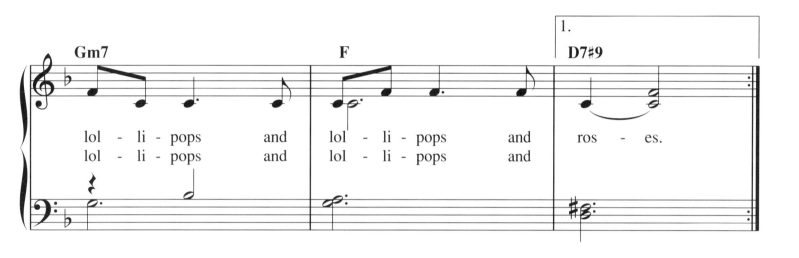

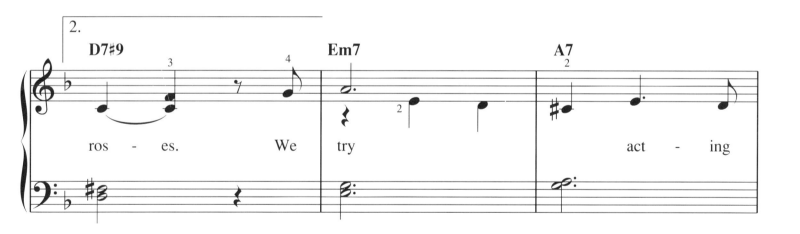

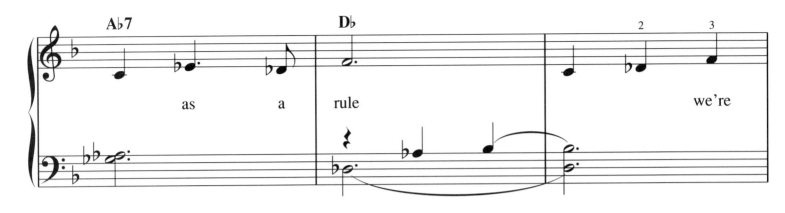

as a rule we're

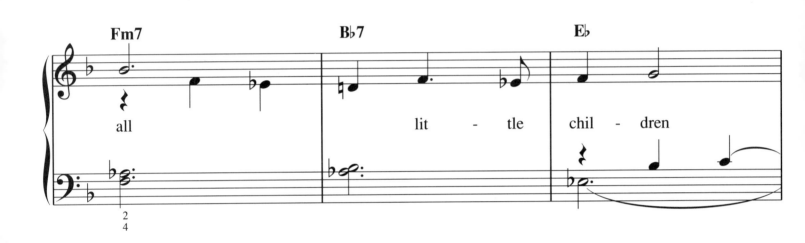

all lit - tle chil - dren

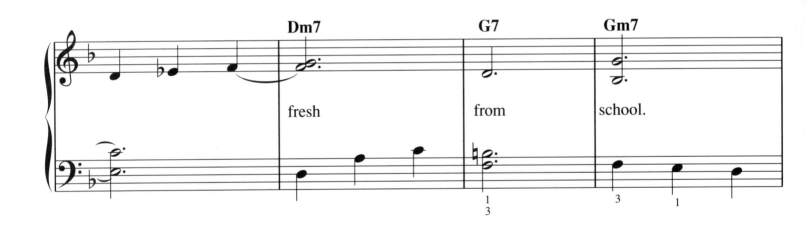

fresh from school.

So car - ry her books. That's how it

61

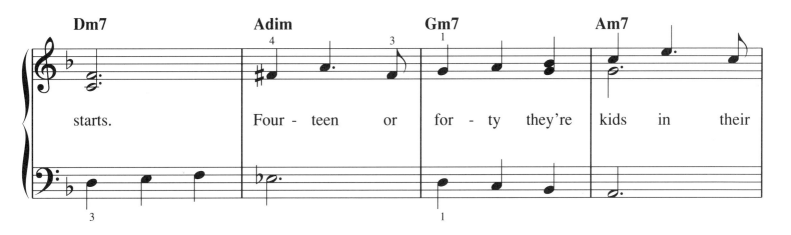

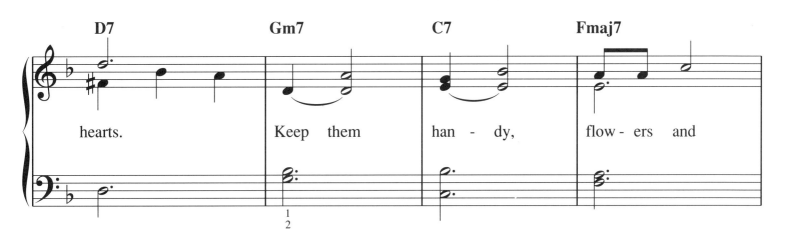

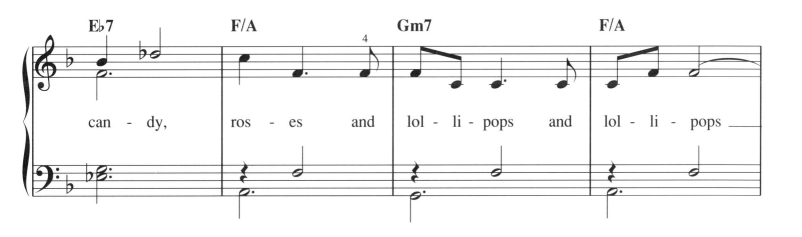

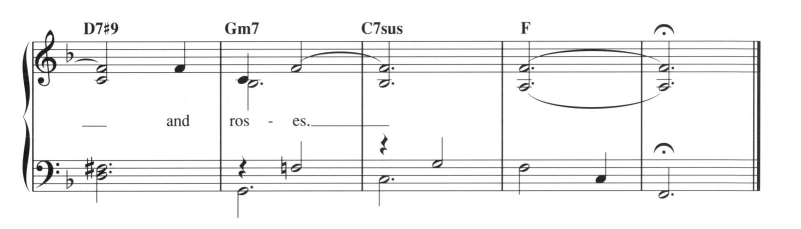

MY IDEAL

from the Paramount Picture PLAYBOY OF PARIS

Words by LEO ROBIN
Music by RICHARD A. WHITING
and NEWELL CHASE

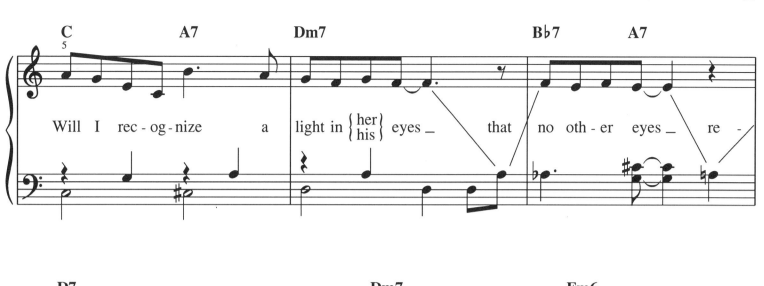

Will I rec-og-nize a light in {her/his} eyes _ that no oth-er eyes _ re-

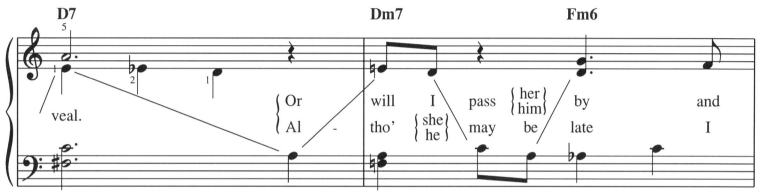

veal. {Or/Al} - {will I/tho'} {she/he} {pass/may} {her/him/be} {by/late} and {/I}

nev - er e - ven know that {she/he} is my i - deal.
trust in fate and so I wait for my i -

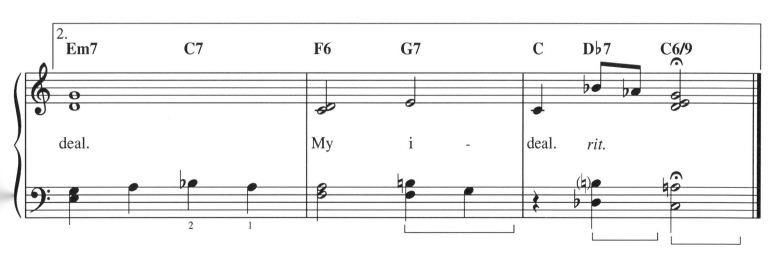

deal. My i - deal. *rit.*

A NIGHTINGALE SANG IN BERKELEY SQUARE

Lyric by ERIC MASCHWITZ
Music by MANNING SHERWIN

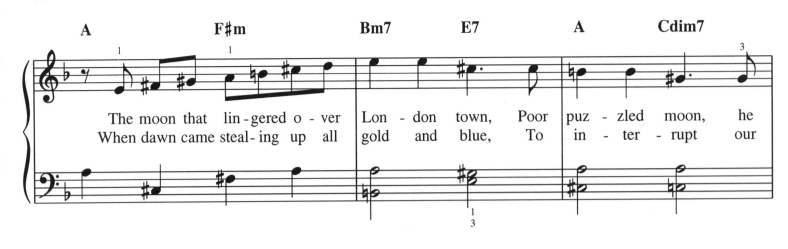

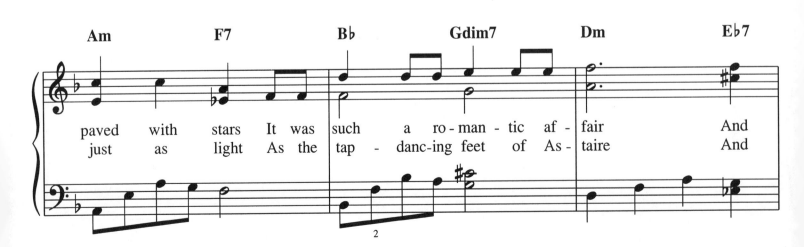

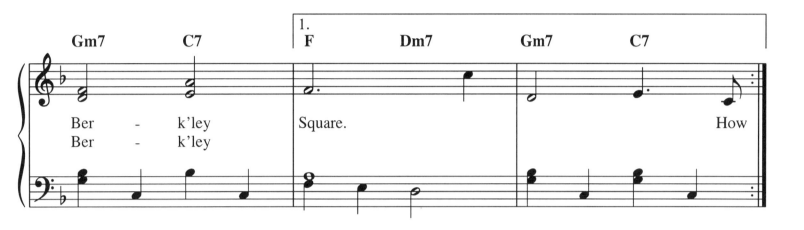

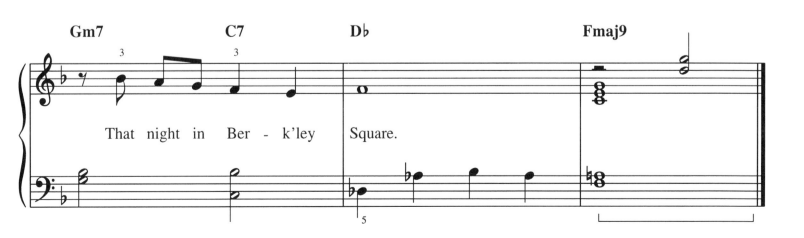

ON A SLOW BOAT TO CHINA

By FRANK LOESSER

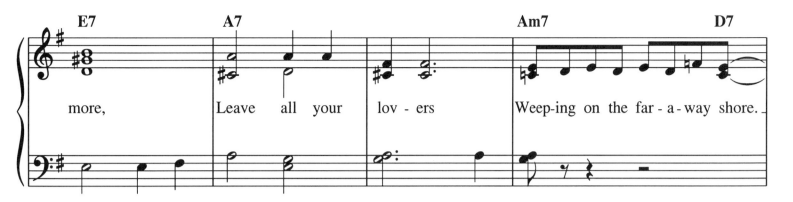

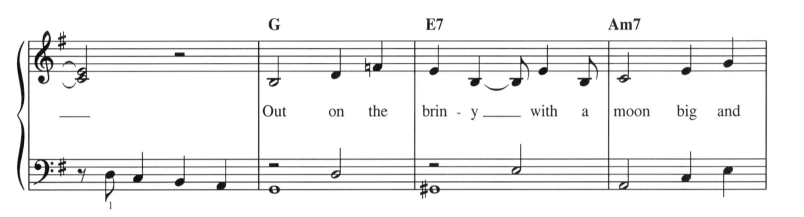

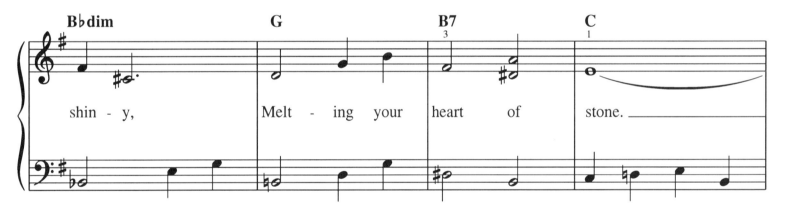

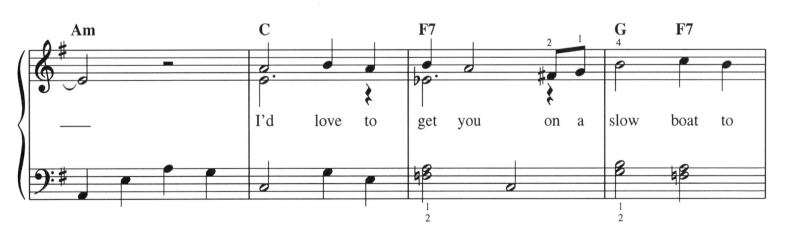

ROCKIN' CHAIR

Words and Music by
HOAGY CARMICHAEL

cab - in, _____ goin' no - where;

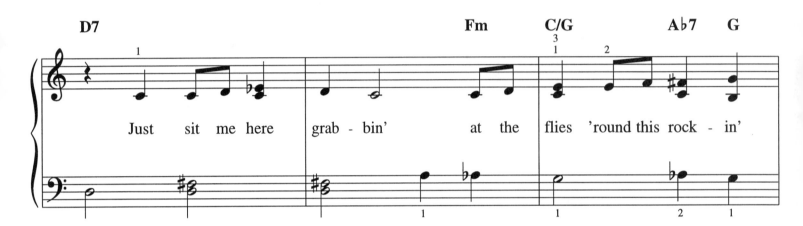

Just sit me here grab - bin' at the flies 'round this rock - in'

chair. My dear old Aunt Har - ri - et

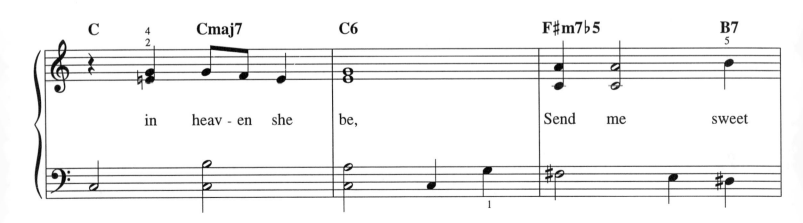

in heav - en she be, Send me sweet

73

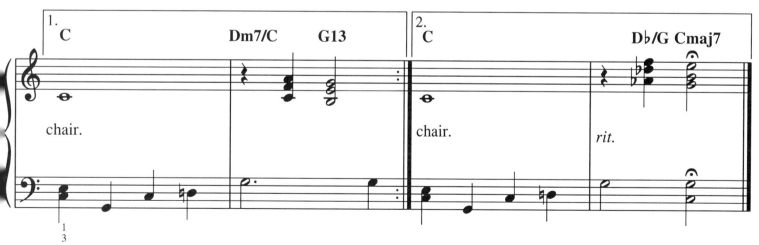

SPRING WILL BE
A LITTLE LATE THIS YEAR

from the Motion Picture CHRISTMAS HOLIDAY

By FRANK LOESSER

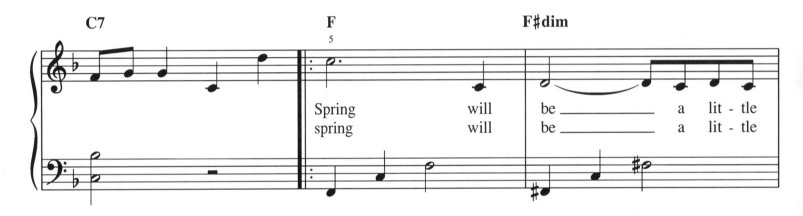

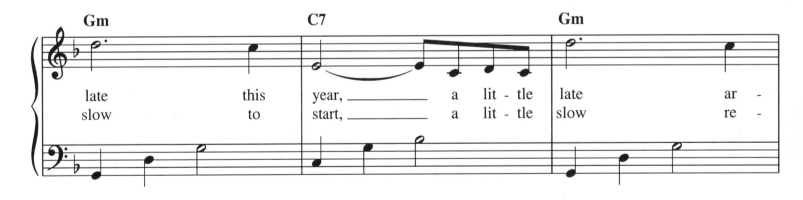

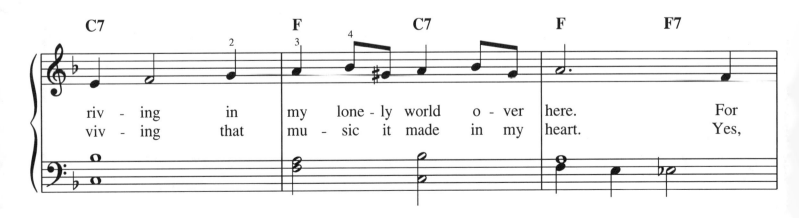

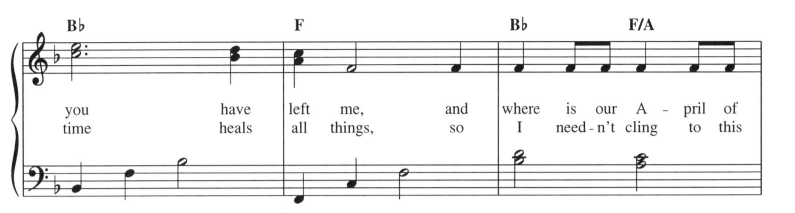

you have left me, and where is our A - pril of
time heals all things, so I need-n't cling to this

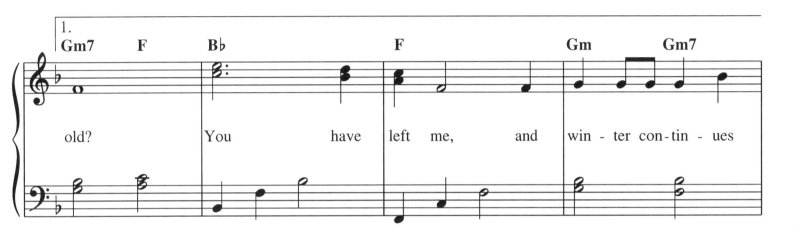

1.
old? You have left me, and win - ter con-tin - ues

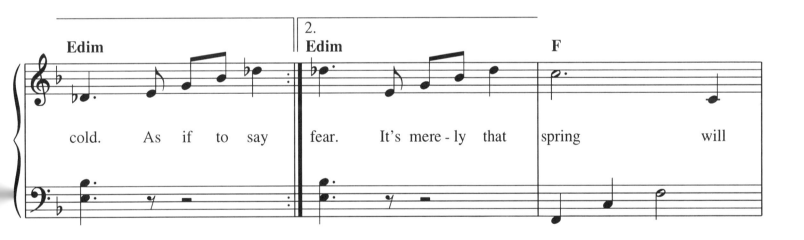

cold. As if to say fear. It's mere-ly that spring will

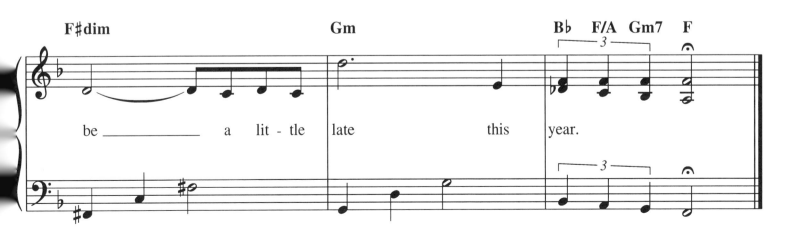

be ____ a lit - tle late this year.

TAKE THE "A" TRAIN

Words and Music by
BILLY STRAYHORN

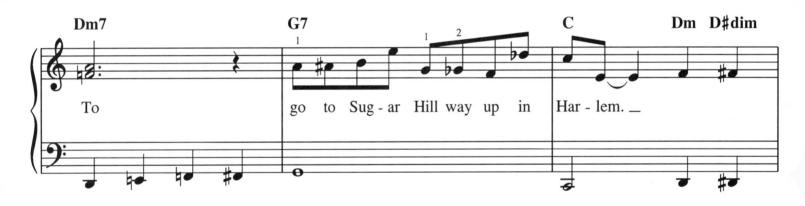

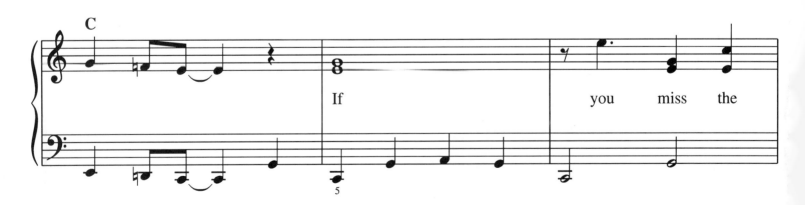

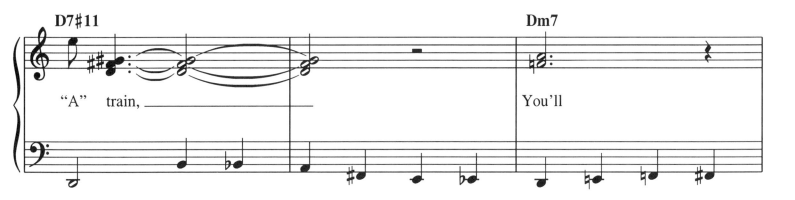

"A" train, _____ You'll

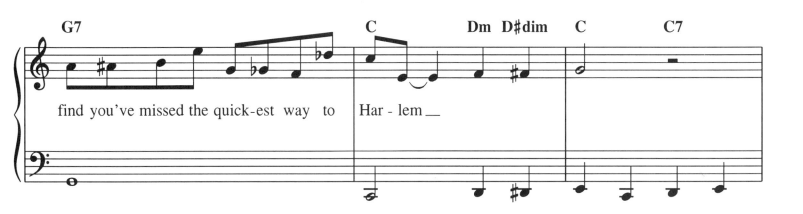

find you've missed the quick-est way to Har - lem ___

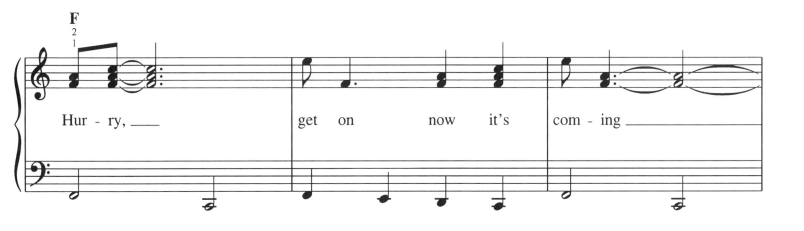

Hur - ry, ___ get on now it's com - ing _____

___ Lis - ten ___ to those rails a -

78

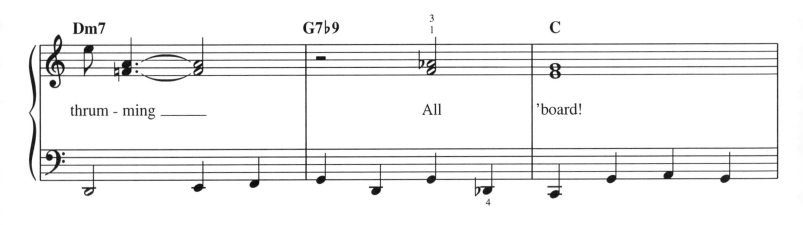

thrum - ming _____   All   'board!

get   on   the   "A"   train _____

Soon   you will be   on Sug - ar Hill in   Har - lem. __

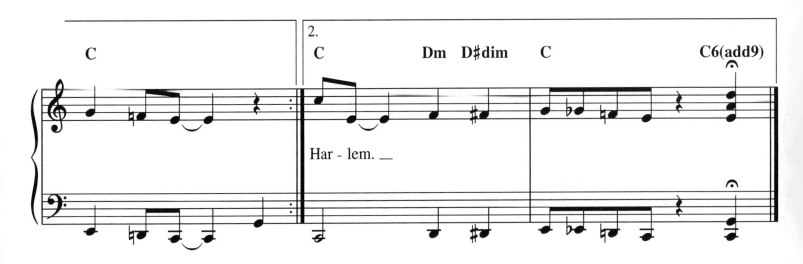

Har - lem. __

TENDERLY

from TORCH SONG

Lyric by JACK LAWRENCE
Music by WALTER GROSS

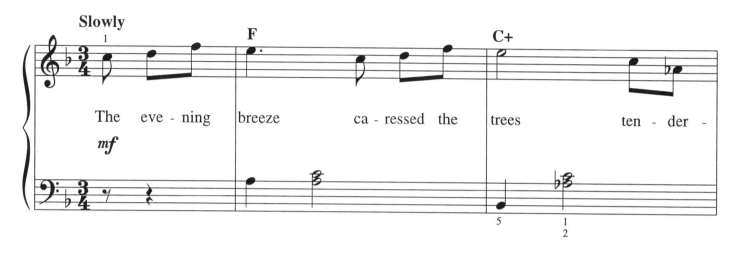

The eve - ning breeze ca - ressed the trees ten - der -

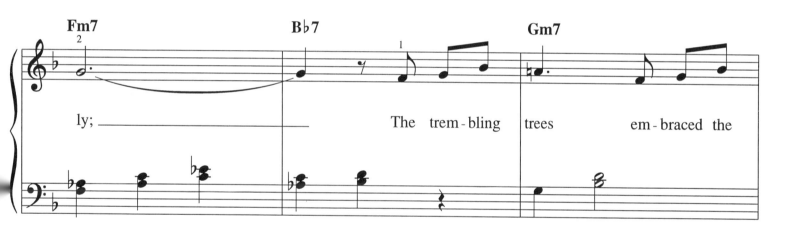

ly; ___ The trem - bling trees em - braced the

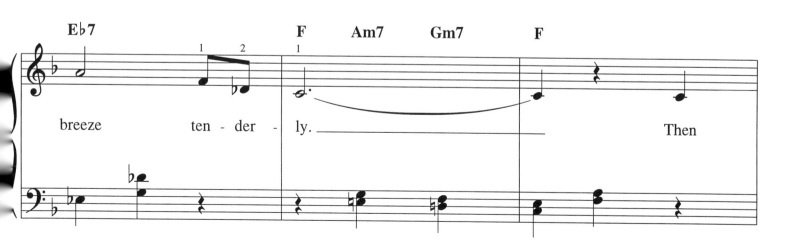

breeze ten - der - ly. ___ Then

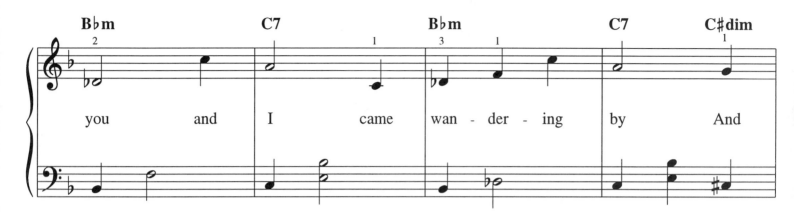

you and I came wan-der-ing by And

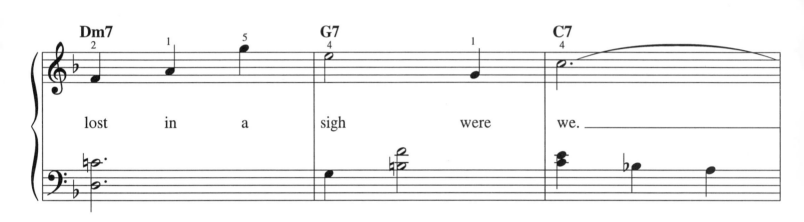

lost in a sigh were we. ____

____ The shore was kissed by sea and mist ten-der-

ly; ____ I can't for-get how two hearts

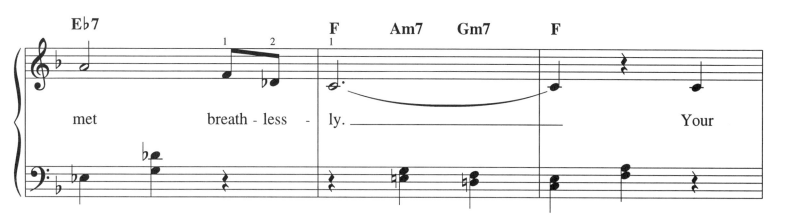

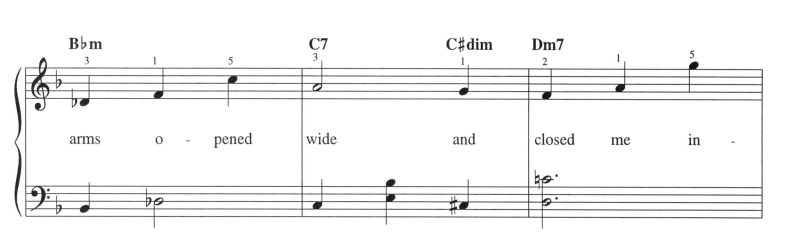

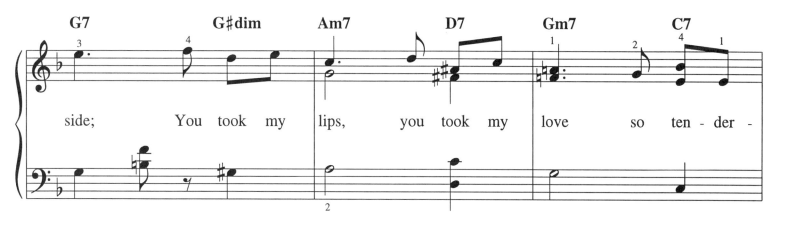

THEY SAY IT'S WONDERFUL
from the Stage Production ANNIE GET YOUR GUN

Words and Music by
IRVING BERLIN

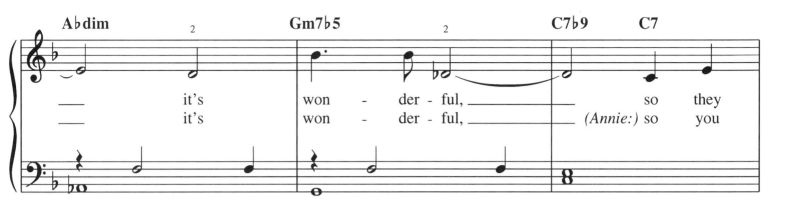

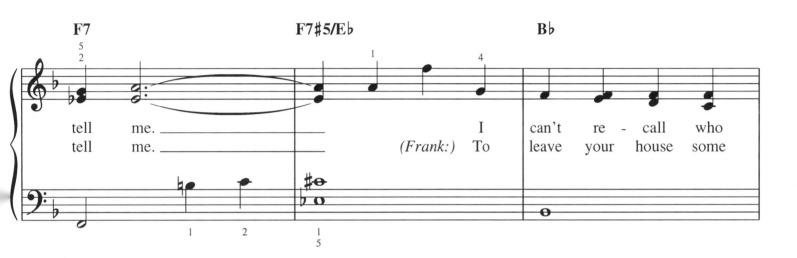

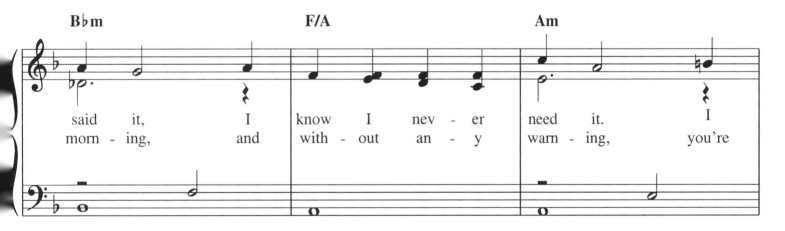

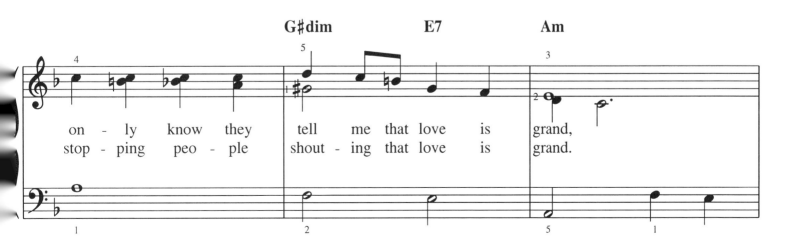

THE VERY THOUGHT OF YOU

Words and Music by
RAY NOBLE

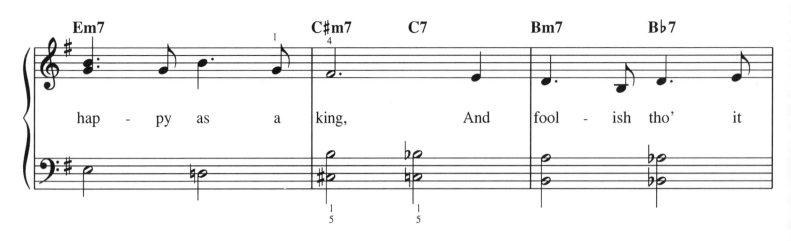

hap - py as a king, And fool - ish tho' it

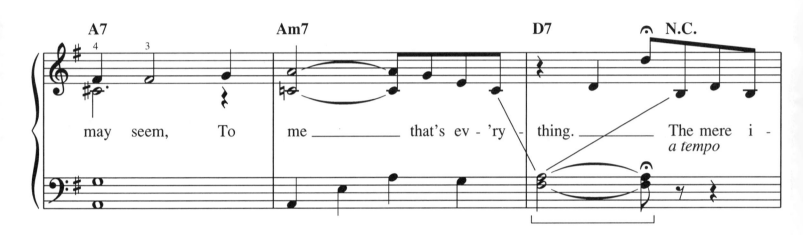

may seem, To me _____ that's ev - 'ry - thing. _____ The mere i -
a tempo

dea of you, The long-ing here for you,

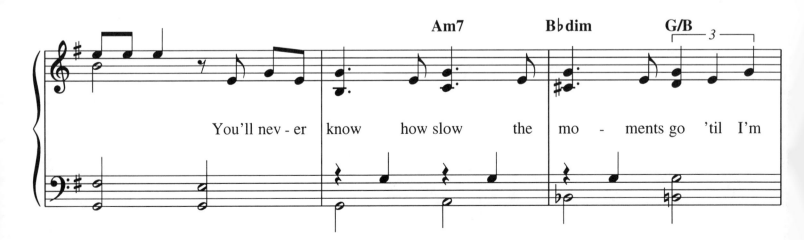

You'll nev - er know how slow the mo - ments go 'til I'm

THE WAY YOU LOOK TONIGHT

from SWING TIME

Words by DOROTHY FIELDS
Music by JEROME KERN

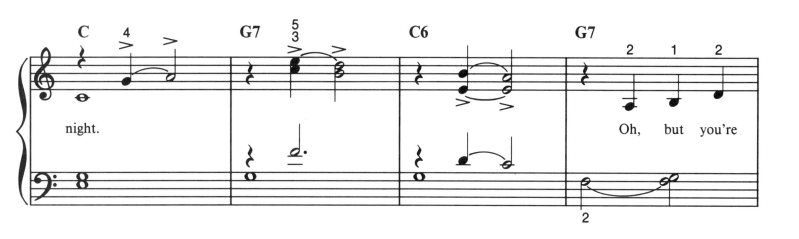

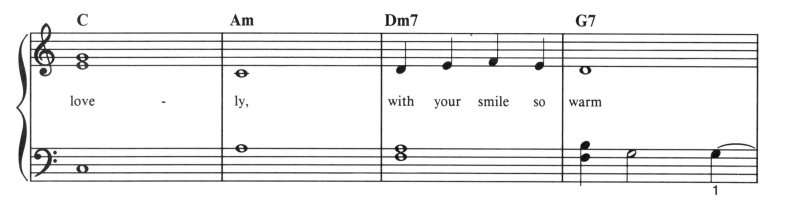

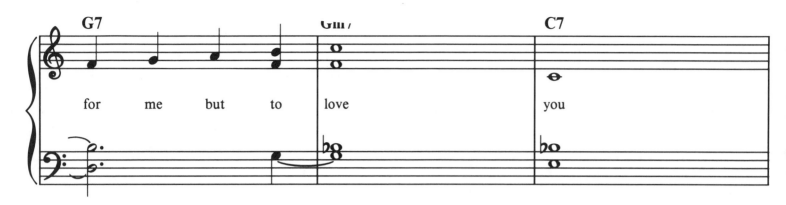

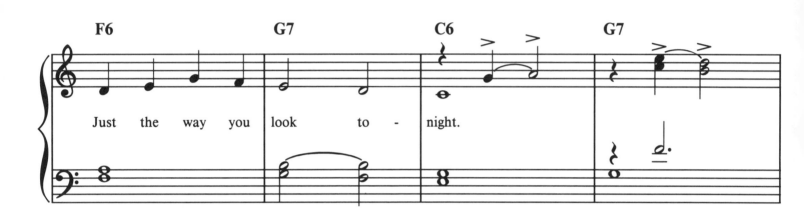

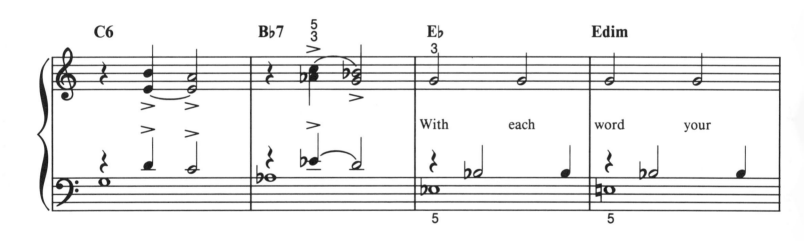

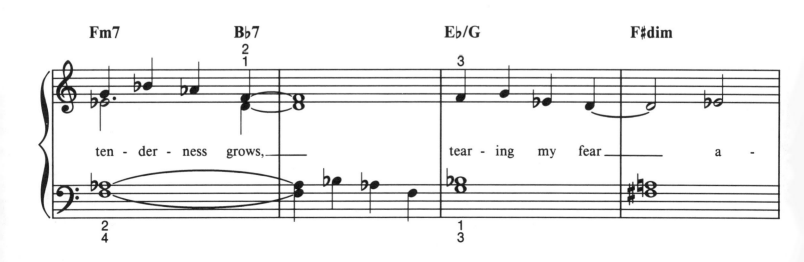

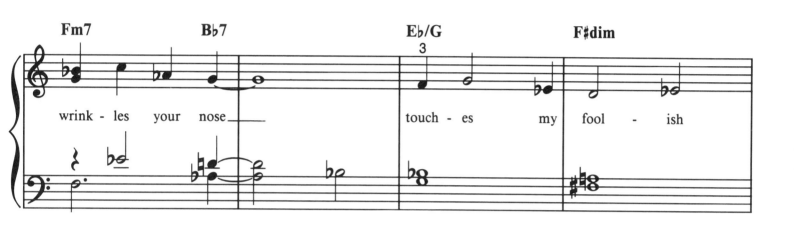

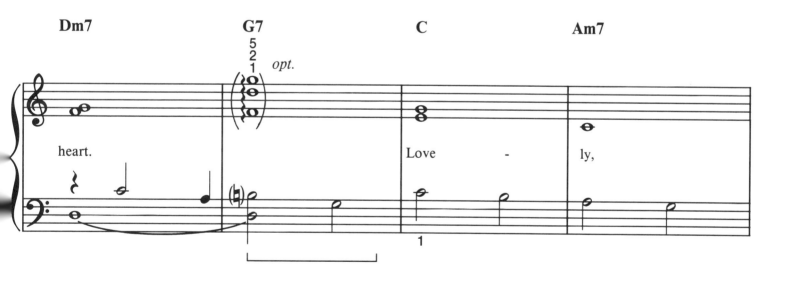

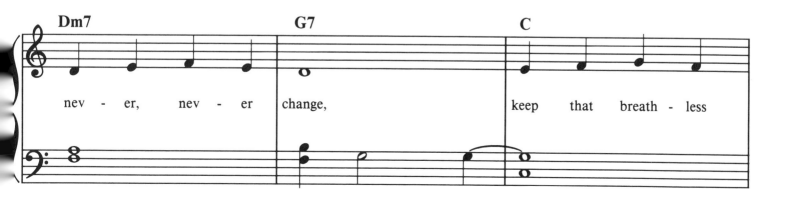

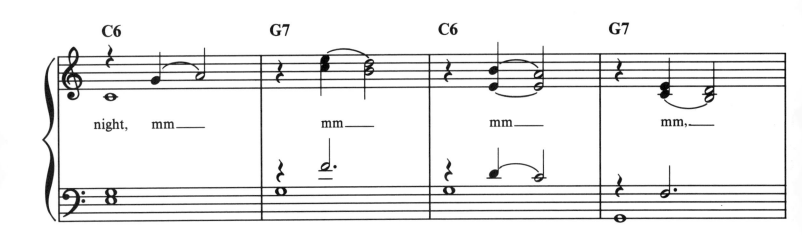

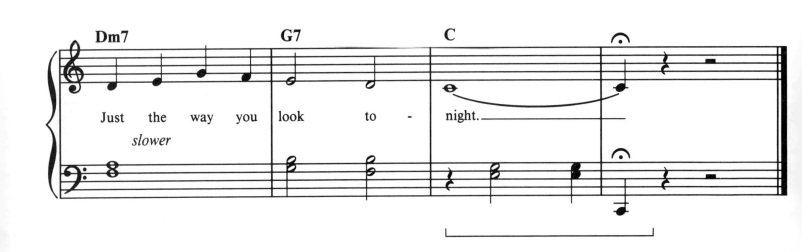

WHAT'S NEW?

Words by JOHNNY BURKE
Music by BOB HAGGART

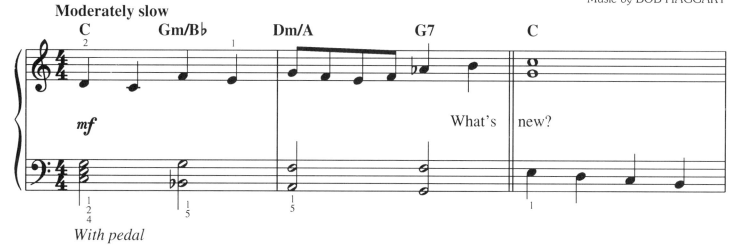

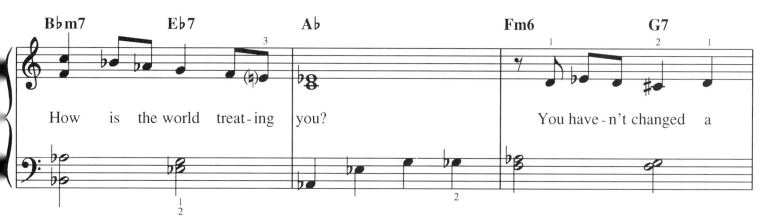

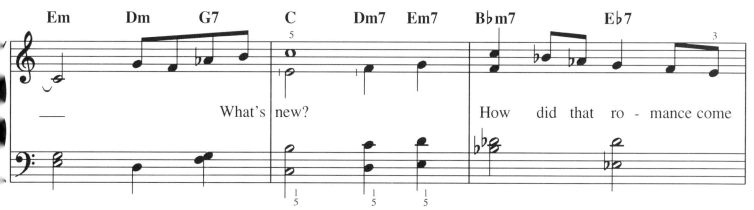

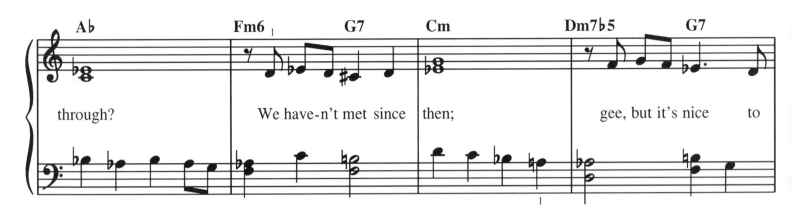

through? | We have-n't met since then; | gee, but it's nice to

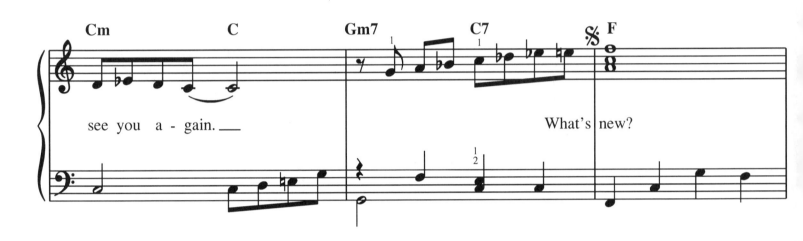

see you a - gain. ___ | What's new?

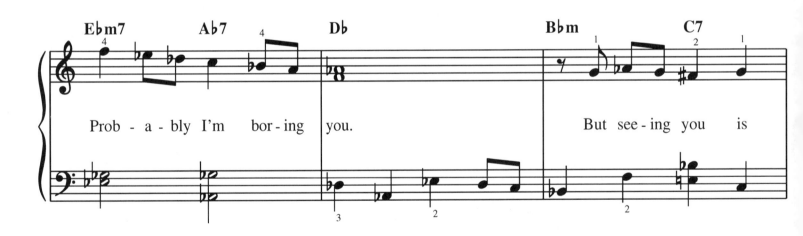

Prob - a - bly I'm bor-ing you. | But see-ing you is

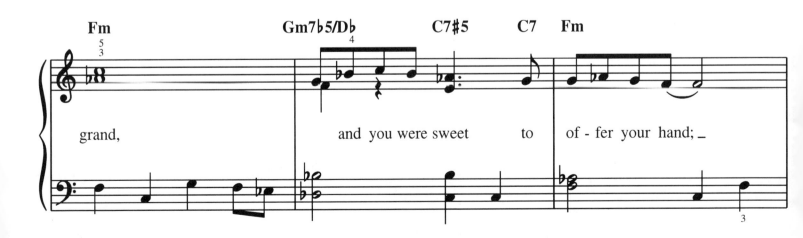

grand, | and you were sweet to | of - fer your hand; ___

It's Easy To Play Your Favorite Songs with Hal Leonard Easy Piano Books

The Best of Today's Movie Hits
16 contemporary film favorites: Change The World • Colors Of The Wind • I Believe In You And Me • I Finally Found Someone • If I Had Words • Mission: Impossible Theme • When I Fall In Love • You Must Love Me • more.
00310248 ....$9.95

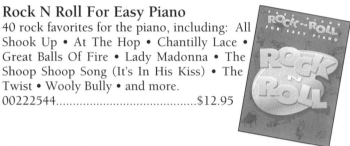

Rock N Roll For Easy Piano
40 rock favorites for the piano, including: All Shook Up • At The Hop • Chantilly Lace • Great Balls Of Fire • Lady Madonna • The Shoop Shoop Song (It's In His Kiss) • The Twist • Wooly Bully • and more.
00222544..$12.95

Playing The Blues
Over 30 great blues tunes arranged for easy piano: Baby, Won't You Please Come Home • Chicago Blues • Fine And Mellow • Heartbreak Hotel • Pinetop's Blues • St. Louis Blues • The Thrill Is Gone • more.
00310102..$12.95

I'll Be Seeing You
50 Songs Of World War II
A salute to the music and memories of WWII, including a chronology of events on the homefront, dozens of photos, and 50 radio favorites of the GIs and their families back home. Includes: Boogie Woogie Bugle Boy • Don't Sit Under The Apple Tree (With Anyone Else But Me) • I Don't Want To Walk Without You • Moonlight In Vermont • and more.
00310147..$17.95

The Best Songs Ever - 3rd Edition
A prestigious collection of 80 all-time favorite songs, featuring: All I Ask Of You • Beauty and the Beast • Body And Soul • Candle In The Wind • Crazy • Don't Know Much • Endless Love • Fly Me To The Moon • The Girl From Ipanema • Here's That Rainy Day • Imagine • In The Mood • Let It Be • Longer • Moonlight In Vermont • People • Satin Doll • Save The Best For Last • Somewhere Out There • Stormy Weather • Strangers In The Night • Tears In Heaven • What A Wonderful World • When I Fall In Love • and more
00359223 ....$19.95

Disney's The Hunchback Of Notre Dame Selections
10 selections from Disney's animated classic, complete with beautiful color illustrations. Includes: The Bells Of Notre Dame • God Help The Outcasts • Out There • Someday • and more.
00316011..$14.95

Country Love Songs
34 classic and contemporary country favorites, including: The Dance • A Few Good Things Remain • Forever And Ever Amen • I Never Knew Love • Love Can Build A Bridge • Love Without End, Amen • She Believes In Me • She Is His Only Need • Where've You Been • and more.
00110030 ....$12.95

Today's Love Songs
31 contemporary favorites, including: All I Ask Of You • Because I Love You • Don't Know Much • Endless Love • Forever And Ever, Amen • Here And Now • I'll Be Loving You Forever • Lost In Your Eyes • Love Without End, Amen • Rhythm Of My Heart • Unchained Melody • Vision Of Love • and more.
00222541..$14.95

R&B Love songs
27 songs, including: Ain't Nothing Like The Real Thing • Easy • Exhale (Shoop Shoop) • The First Time Ever I Saw Your Face • Here And Now • I'm Your Baby Tonight • My Girl • Never Can Say Goodbye • Ooo Baby Baby • Save The Best For Last • Someday • Still • and more.
00310181 Easy Piano......................$12.95

Best Of Cole Porter
Over 30 songs, including: Be A Clown • Begin The Beguine • Easy To Love • From This Moment On • In The Still Of The Night • Night And Day • So In Love • Too Darn Hot • You Do Something To Me • You'd Be So Nice To Come Home To • and more
00311576..$14.95

FOR MORE INFORMATION, SEE YOUR LOCAL MUSIC DEALER,
OR WRITE TO:

HAL•LEONARD®
CORPORATION
7777 W. BLUEMOUND RD. P.O. BOX 13819 MILWAUKEE, WI 53213

Prices, book contents, and availability subject to change without notice

0597